An experienced mission executive of a globe-girdling ministry has written
a remarkable handbook for anyone seriously interested
in seeing the timely completion of the task of missions. This is the first
book on global mission strategy to have successfully
made the paradigm shift from "winning souls in all countries" to
thinking consistently in terms of "planting pioneer church movements in
all of the remaining Unreached People Groups."

RALPH D. WINTER,
general director, U.S. Center for World Mission

Our Lord prophesied that the good news of the gospel would be preached
in the whole world as a witness to all people groups (Mt 24:14).
Penetrating Missions' Final Frontier shows how this can be done in
today's world not only through fully supported
missionaries but also through those who like the apostle Paul are
tentmakers or self-supporting professionals. In the first Reformation the
people of God were given the Word of God. This book
shows that we need another Reformation where the people of God are
given the work of God in order to complete Christ's commission.

J. CHRISTY WILSON JR.,
emeritus professor of world evangelization,
Gordon-Conwell Theological Seminary

When Ted writes, it is a marriage between his brilliant, analytical mind
and his compassionate heart. This book is a manual
for a new missionary movement. It lays the foundation for a practical
and tactical way to see our whole globe reached with the gospel.

FRANK KALEB JANSEN,
executive director, Adopt-A-People Clearinghouse

This is a definitive book on missions. It is well-researched, biblical, practical, holistic and achievable. It is a welcome call to renewal for the laity and professionals as God's Special Envoys to penetrate missions' final frontier. It advocates a symbiotic approach to fulfill our task to "make disciples of all the nations" for Christ, a strategy that the churches cannot afford to ignore.

AUGUSTIN B. VENCER JR.,
international director, World Evangelical Fellowship

Ted presents the reader with a fresh, well-documented, practical challenge for penetrating the final frontier of unreached peoples. He builds a strong case for the need for creative new approaches to launch thousands upon thousands of "God's Special Envoys" to penetrate the remaining unreached peoples.

LUIS BUSH,
international director, AD 2000 & Beyond Movement

The strategy in Dr. Yamamori's book is truly realistic and innovative. This challenging study calls for the rise of a new generation of mission elite as God's special envoys. I highly recommend this book.

TADATAKA MARUYAMA,
president, Tokyo Christian University

TETSUNAO YAMAMORI

PENETRATING
MISSIONS'
FINAL FRONTIER

- A NEW
  STRATEGY
  FOR
  UNREACHED
  PEOPLES

Foreword by
Dan Harrison

INTERVARSITY PRESS
DOWNERS GROVE, ILLINOIS 60515

InterVarsity Press® is the book-publishing division of InterVarsity Christian Fellowship®, a student movement active on campus at hundreds of universities, colleges and schools of nursing in the United States of America, and a member movement of the International Fellowship of Evangelical Students. For information about local and regional activities, write Public Relations Dept., InterVarsity Christian Fellowship, 6400 Schroeder Rd., P.O. Box 7895, Madison, WI 53707-7895.

Author royalties from the sale of this book have been designated for the relief and development work of Food for the Hungry, Inc. These funds will support symbiotic ministry to help fight the two hungers—of the body and of the soul.

The author gratefully acknowledges permission to reprint The Lausanne Covenant from John R. W. Stott's Lausanne Occasional Papers, No. 3: The Lausanne Covenant—An Exposition and Commentary (Wheaton: Lausanne Committee for World Evangelization 1975; first published by World Wide Publications, Minneapolis: 1975). He also gratefully acknowledges permission to reprint "An Appeal to Disciples Everywhere" (Adopt-A-People Clearinghouse).

This book incorporates portions of God's New Envoys, originally published by Multonomah Press, 1987. It also contains selections from "God's Special Envoys," originally presented by the author as a commencement address at William Carey International University, and published in Mission Frontiers (Pasadena: U.S. Center for World Mission), August-September 1985, pp. 9-11.

Cover illustration: Roberta Polfus

ISBN: 0-8308-1370-5

Printed in the United States of America ∞

Library of Congress Cataloging-in-Publication Data

Yamamori, Tetsunao, 1937-
   Penetrating missions' final frontier: a new strategy for
unreached peoples/Tetsunao Yamamori: foreword by Dan Harrison.
     p. cm.
   Includes bibliographical references (p.   ) and index.
   ISBN 0-8308-1370-5
   1. Missions—Theory. I. Title. II. Title: Unreached peoples.
BV2063.Y363   1993   93-35651
266—dc20   CIP

15 14 13 12 11 10 9 8 7 6 5 4 3 2 1

04 03 02 01 00 99 98 97 96 95 94 93

*Dedicated to all those individuals,
churches and organizations that would dare remain
faithful to the Great Commission
until Missions' Final Frontier is penetrated—
when the last unreached peoples are brought
to faith and obedience in Christ.*

Part 4/Taking the First Step

Appendixes

Reader Response Card

"For the Word of God is living and active.
Sharper than any double-edged sword,
it penetrates even to dividing soul
and spirit,
joints and marrow;
it judges the thoughts and attitudes
of the heart.
Nothing in all creation
is hidden from God's sight."
HEBREWS 4:12-13

Maps, Charts and Diagrams

Foreword

No country is closed to God; yet nearly four billion people have still not accepted Christ as Lord and Savior. Dr. Ted Yamamori's book, *Penetrating Missions' Final Frontier,* explores this dilemma.

The author challenges the worldwide church with a paradigm shift: send 600,000 tentmakers *in addition* to traditional missionaries. A tentmaker is a person who has all the spiritual depth and scriptural knowledge of a traditional missionary, but serves vocationally in another professional capacity. Perhaps she's a doctor or an entrepreneur. He may be a teacher or an engineer. This book helps us Christians realize how many opportunities we have for mission work no matter what the political climate is.

This is 1993. Ayatollah Khomeini is dead. Former Communists have torn down the Berlin wall. The Soviet Union, Yugoslavia and Czechoslovakia have disintegrated into new republics, anxious for technological and economic development. Somalia and the Sudan are shattered by civil wars. Their citizens may have spiritual questions, but the governments know they need food, political stability, clean water, efficient transportation systems, competent physicians, creative professors. Tentmakers are very welcome in these countries. These cataclysmic changes provoked Dr. Yamamori to write this book.

Ted Yamamori has thoroughly researched those parts of the world which lack both basic physical necessities and a viable, indigenous church. Under what circumstances would a fundamentalist Islamic country accept an American Christian, a Korean Christian or a Costa Rican Christian? What about mainland China? Nepal, where it has been a crime to change your religion? Secular Libya? Communist Cuba? Islamic Malaysia?

No country is closed to a loving God. Years ago, when Western missionaries were denied access to the Soviet Union, African believers traveled to the USSR and the East bloc. How? They went for college. While studying, they spread news of the gospel. Gradually, the East bloc opened up to other Christians from around the world—they came as teachers, as engineers, as students, as businesspeople. Winning legitimate entree to the "creative access" world through excellent service and exemplary character, these believers naturally had opportunities to speak about their faith.

These are the people Ted Yamamori talks about in the book you hold. People like Dwight and Mary Nordstrom who served God in mainland China—he as an executive with an international corporation; she as a medical doctor. Ted Yamamori knows that it's not "business as usual" in the modern world of missions. Under his leadership, Food for the Hungry has instituted unique programs that send international workers to serve with indigenous agencies to help them accomplish their own goals, working toward their sense of what's needed in their countries. What better way for you to serve with integrity?

If you want to know how to serve God in the most needy of the unreached parts of this creative access world, consider the kind of opportunities that are described in this book. Less than 10 percent of all missionaries and Christian workers work in these countries without an indigenous church. Won't you consider joining the few Christians who will affect so many?

Dan Harrison
Director of Missions and Urbana
InterVarsity Christian Fellowship

Preface

This book presents a bold new strategy for effectively evangelizing the thousands of people groups that still lack a viable Christian presence in their midst. The specific focus of this strategy is the unreached peoples that share both of the two most basic human needs. These are the *physical* need for adequate food, clean water and reasonable health, and the *spiritual* need for salvation through Jesus Christ. Without our immediate help, these groups face a terrifying double jeopardy—continual suffering in this world and eternal suffering in the world to come.

In the pages that follow, you will learn about a new mission elite that will be raised up and trained to employ this new strategy. They will penetrate these doubly-at-risk groups—healing them physically, socially and mentally, and opening their hearts for Christ.

You will also be briefed on the new global mission context, learning about the opportunities, challenges and exciting new resources that it includes. In the process, you will learn where *you* fit into this global movement. Perhaps you will be inspired to become deeply involved.

The strategy presented in this book is flexible and ubiquitous. Individuals can participate in many different ways. This strategy will enhance many different kinds of global evangelization plans.

With God's help, and in partnership with other plans, this strategy will help bring the gospel to the most resistant and the most hurting of the still unreached peoples—helping to penetrate *missions' final frontier.*

That's the overview. Details follow!

Acknowledgments

I must thank many individuals. Dr. Dan Harrison and Paula Harrison Esealuka of InterVarsity Christian Fellowship encouraged me to write this book in time for Urbana 93. Andy Le Peau, the editorial director of InterVarsity Press, joined the team of encouragers. With my already crowded schedule, I was vacillating on my decision. Some on the Board of Directors of Food for the Hungry, namely Mr. Friedrich Hanssler, Mr. Frank Consalvo, and Dr. Akira Horiuchi, individually counseled me to take on the challenge. Without their gentle but firm nudge I probably would not have done so.

Not living with research data as I used to as an academician, I knew I had to depend on those who did, and they were most cooperative and kind in assisting me. In no special order, I wish to acknowledge them for providing me with new data, fresh insights and professional courtesy: Dr. Ralph Winter, Frank Kaleb Jansen, Luis Bush, Dr. David Barrett, Patrick Johnstone, Warren Lawrence, Dr. Christy Wilson Jr., Todd Johnson, Don Hamilton, Pete Holzmann, Dr. Kitty Purgason, Kathy Giskie, Dr. John Cragin, Dr. Jay Lykins, James Stephens, Dr. Gordon Loux, Berry Fiess and Chris Woehr.

An extra word of appreciation is due to Douglas S. Jardine, a Ph.D. candidate in sociology at Arizona State University. Doug is a brilliant scholar-in-the-making. I worked with him before, and his research and editorial assistance for this project was indispensable.

During the six months of this project I have caused inconvenience to some of the staff members at Food for the Hungry for not being readily accessible and have burdened others with additional assignments. I have appreciated their cheerful compliance. My gratitude goes to Amy McClain, Esther Niles, Debbie Pearson and Lisa Leff for their manuscript typing and artwork.

In this project and others before it, my family has suffered from my inadvertent neglect, which they have accepted with understanding. I wish to thank Judy, Kelli and Steven for their ever enthusiastic support of me and my work. My love to all of them. Judy, who has stood by me all these years of our marriage and my professional life, has functioned not only as my sounding board on project ideas but also as the "editor-in-chief" of most of my writings, constantly demanding lucidity of thought and clarity of expression from them. I want to recognize her publicly, despite her desire to remain anonymous.

Introduction
The Opportunity!

No GENERATION BEFORE US HAS EVER BEEN POISED IN FRONT of so great an opportunity. While global problems and population are well known to be escalating constantly, the counterbalancing but less-known fact is that the forces of Christianity and specifically the results of mission outreach in this century have combined to reduce the number of non-Christians per serious Christian believer from a ratio of 50 to 1 in 1900 to less than 7 to 1 in 1994, and that ratio continues to drop.

The Soviet Union and China have long represented the two largest land masses and also major population blocs determinedly working with ruthless totalitarian methods to reduce the number of Christians accessible to them. Yet despite this hostility the Christian movements in both places have grown irresistibly, and in China enormously.

Today the Soviet Union has collapsed, throwing open the doors to formerly inaccessible nationalities that we could almost have despaired of ever reaching. With the "vast new army of at least 100,000 missionaries and paramissionaries who have since flooded into the former USSR and Eastern Europe,"[1] many of these former Communists may be saved. Yet even with this astounding and unexpected opening for the gospel, there will still be a massive and *growing* body of non-Christians in the world—utterly outside the reaches of traditional missionary approaches.[2]

The same could soon be true for China. But this does not automatically mean that we will be ready to move into this flood of new areas with both competence and commensurate strength.

Three obstacles require our attention:

Poor targeting. Churches are sadly given to meeting their own needs. As David Barrett and Todd Johnson demonstrate so eloquently, the already-Christian world is focusing up to 99.9 percent of its resources on itself, leaving only a tenth of one percent for evangelizing the billions of non-Christians outside of predominantly Christian lands. The actual figures are that the Christian world receives 99 percent of all Christian literature, 90.9 percent of all foreign missionaries, 95 percent of all full-time Christian workers and 99.9 percent of all output from Christian radio/TV. Even overseas "mission field" churches are clamoring for mission funds for their own local needs while mission vision for the fields still beyond receives only about 10 percent of mission monies and personnel. We must press for a greater shift toward the unreached peoples.

Key specialists missing. While the current categories of mission specialists will always be needed, new kinds of specialists are needed, and in large numbers. In particular, the mission work force needs men and women who are trained to penetrate people groups that are highly resistant to the gospel, and where the quality of life is exceptionally low. Increasingly, these are exactly the characteristics of the groups where the vast majority of the unreached are found.[3]

New strategic shift needed. To evangelize the dwindling number of unreached people groups effectively, we welcome the many new approaches that are being tried out this very moment. But we must deliberately continue this strategic shift,

or the vast new array of opportunities will go wanting.
Obviously these are big problems, and to be resolved they will require broad cooperation between many Christians and many Christian organizations. But today over a hundred mission agencies are working together in "strategic partnerships" catalyzed by InterDev, and thousands of Christian leaders are working in harmony in relation to the AD 2000 and Beyond Movement.

Our Response

This book emphasizes a current shift in strategy that singles out and targets the people groups least likely to be reached with present mission deployment and emphasis. This strategy—which I call *contextual symbiosis*—also accommodates both the physical needs and the spiritual hostility of many of these groups.

I propose to include in the strategy I am describing a new emphasis on the identification and training of a specific breed of missionaries I could call "God's Special Envoys." They are indeed special, in that they are specially selected and trained to emphasize the mission methods that have proven themselves in causing the percentage of Christians in the world to increase rapidly, growing at an average of roughly three times the growth rate of the world population.

It is not this book's intent that the numbers of traditional missionaries be reduced. Their steadfast efforts have explored many of the ideas emphasized in this book. We can hope that existing mission efforts will continue to increase in strength, while at the same time the necessary shift in emphasis we are describing will grow as well.

The goal, as always, is obedience to our Lord's Great Commission:

Be my witnesses . . . to the ends of the earth. (Acts 1:8) Go into all the world and preach the good news to all creation. (Mk 16:15)

Go and make disciples of all nations, baptizing them in the name of the Father and of the Son and of the Holy Spirit, and teaching them to obey everything I have commanded you. (Mt 28:19-20)[4]

There is no ignoring the binding and urgent nature of these commands. So one additional objective of this book is to mobilize Christians who have mistakenly seen the Great Commission as voluntary.

This book is primarily for . . .

• students, professionals and other skilled and dedicated people who might qualify to be or become one of God's Special Envoys.

• pastors, ministers, teachers, mission executives and others who are charged to encourage and counsel those planning missionary careers.

• all those concerned with Christian relief and development work—who seek better ways to meet physical, mental and social needs, while increasing the harvest for Christ.

Finally, I have written this book to assist the nearly 325,000 missionaries—hailing from many parts of the earth—who already labor in the field so valiantly.[5] I hope they will find this Special-Envoy, contextual-symbiosis strategy adaptable to much of the work they are doing now, and that at least some of the ideas will give them reinforcement, encouragement and guidance.

Throughout these pages you will find examples of God's Special Envoys in action, illustrating different situations they will encounter and the techniques they can employ. Many of these examples are drawn from case studies of traditional missionaries who, in the situations illustrated, are responding as Special Envoys would in the face of such challenges. Other examples relate to current Special Envoys, whether or not they have begun to call themselves by that name. All of the examples are based on experiences of real missionaries in real-world situations. The occasional alteration of names and locations is designed to protect missionaries and converts who are in areas where Christian witness places them at physical risk.

A Personal Word

As you journey through this book, you may find it helpful to know a little more about the author who accompanies you.

To begin, you should know that the topics discussed in this book are profoundly important to me. In different forms they have been the focus of my entire life. Over the past forty years I have been studying church growth and mission strategies, first as a student, then as a university professor. I have also been writing about them in articles and books.

Recently my involvement in global evangelism has taken a different turn. Since 1981 I have led a Christian relief and development organization, the goal of which is to minister in our Lord's name to the physical and spiritual needs of suffering people in desperately needy areas of the world. This experience, like the ones before, has strengthened my conviction that the Great Commission can be pursued with far greater effectiveness.

I am sure that part of the motivation for this book, as with all of my mission writings, comes from the fact that I myself was once counted among the "foreign" nonbelievers we seek to reach. Thus for me the needs of the unreached will always be very real, as will their pain.

In my case, that pain became acute the last year of World War II, when I was seven and lived in Japan's third largest city, Nagoya. I was raised as a Buddhist and Shintoist and was taught to look to Buddha for support and to worship nature spirits and my ancestors. During that time I watched three bombs fall within the gates of our home and saw a family member killed. As a result, even though I was a child, I began to think deeply about human suffering and the possibility for true world peace.

At that time I also experienced physical hunger. Like some of those described in this book, I was one of the millions of children whose food supply was disrupted by war. In fact, if the shortages in Nagoya had continued much longer, I probably would have starved to death. Those early memories and the deadly effects of war never left me. They remain strong even today.

After things got better, I attended Jesuit schools—respected in my country for their high educational standards. I was still, however, not a believer.

Then another war—this time in Korea—brought a United States Air Force chaplain to Nagoya. As I got to know the Vernon Kullowatz family, I began thinking that there was something different about them.

Through this family I began attending church. I wanted to know more about the God who sent Jesus Christ. I also volunteered to work for the Kullowatzes as a houseboy to see if their belief was practiced at home. It was.

Soon I started reading the Bible the Kullowatzes had given me. I began to seek a career in the diplomatic corps, where I hoped to make a contribution to world peace.[6]

As with most conversions, the rest is something of a mystery. I came to understand that the diplomatic corps was not the answer—and that the only lasting peace for the world would come as "we have peace with God through our Lord Jesus Christ" (Rom 5:1).

While at Nanzan University, I discovered I wanted to learn more about God's Word, to learn to be a "workman . . . who correctly handles the word of truth" (2 Tim 2:15). The first step, I knew, was to establish "vertical" peace through a direct saving relationship with God in Jesus Christ. Only after that, I believed, could the true "horizontal" peace follow, in which neighbors love neighbors as themselves.

Having at last found my direction, I could not be stopped. I studied Bible in one college, received a divinity degree from another, became a Christian minister, and completed a doctorate in sociology of religion. This led to teaching, writing and Christian relief/development work.

Then, after a while, came the present endeavor—which you and I can pursue together on the following pages, as we explore a new strategy and a new mobilization of human energy for the year 2000 and beyond.

PART 1
Background

1
Our
Mandate
for the
Global Mission

The FUNDAMENTAL REASON FOR EMPHASIZING A MAJOR shift to what I am calling a contextual-symbiosis, Special-Envoy strategy is that this is the most likely emphasis that can allow us to complete the task of reaching all the unreached peoples in a relatively short time.

Even a century ago the completion of the task was not unthinkable. From the late 1800s through the first few years of the 1900s, many mission strategists believed that the world could be evangelized before the twentieth century drew to a close. As David B. Barrett states:

> By the year 1900, one third of humanity were Christians, and one half were aware of Christianity and had become influenced by it. Optimism for rapid completion of the task of global evangelization was high. From 1889 to 1914 the great Protestant and Anglican communions of Europe and North

America promoted the Watchword that summarized this optimism in the objective, "The Evangelization of the World in This Generation."[1]

While these optimistic projections were not entirely realized, the impact of that generation and the strategizing they did stands as a marvelous impetus to us today to act with equal decisiveness in a situation that is on the order of ten times as bright!

Many bewail the falling percentage of global population constituted by the population of the Western world, where birth control and abortion combine to reduce population growth almost to zero. And thus it would appear that Christians the world over are also declining. But in actual fact the miracle is that the small, fledgling Christian communities in Africa, Latin America and Asia have grown so much in this century, and are growing so fast right now, that the global percentage of Christians has actually held steady throughout this century. While both Christians and non-Christians in the Western world have moved to smaller families, non-Western Christians have not only grown as fast as their non-Christian neighbors, but with evangelization going on at almost unheard of rates—from two to five times the general population growth rate—their growth has more than compensated for "the decline of the West."

As we face the end of the current century, it is essential to understand clearly just what has and has not worked, and to pour our resources resolutely into those approaches that stand the greatest chance of continuing this marvelous century of growth. At the beginning of the century 10 percent of evangelicals were in the "mission lands." Now more than 70 percent of them are. Let us keep in mind that Bible-believing Christians began the century as one out of fifty in the world's population, and that we are now one out of ten. But to conserve and fulfill the godly, sacrificial labors of the past, there are certain things we must do. To begin, we need to take two steps: first, to define our terms, so we can focus our investigation more precisely; second, to review why we should devote our time, perhaps even our lives, to evangelizing in foreign lands.

Definition of Terms and the New Mission Targeting Aids
Throughout this book I will use a handful of key words repeatedly as I describe the process central to our purpose—bringing people from other cultures to faith and obedience in Christ. Brief definitions of these terms will be sufficient for us here. As you read through these terms, please remember that they will provide the basis for your understanding of the new mission context. So take your time and make sure you understand them before going on to the next chapter.

In this same section, you will also encounter some of the newest informational tools available for targeting the global mission effort. Through the generosity of their creators, you may be seeing some of them in these pages, even before they are published by those who have spent so many years creating them. As you will learn, this kind of sharing and selflessness is quite typical of the current mission context.

*   *   *

The first of the basic terms, *evangelization,* is specifically related to proclamation of the gospel. According to the helpful definition in the *World Christian Encyclopedia,* being evangelized refers to "the state of having the good news spread or offered; the state of being aware of Christianity, Christ and the gospel."[2]

Evangelism, for our purposes, does *not* mean conversion. Rather, it would seem to be exactly what Jesus had in mind when he told the disciples to "Go into all the world and preach the good news to all creation" (Mk 16:15). An evangelized country is one in which more than half the members have had an opportunity to hear or read some of the key elements of the gospel. They have not necessarily been converted.[3]

A second concept has to do with whether or not a people group is *reached.* To qualify to be reached, there must be a viable indigenous church "with adequate numbers and resources to evangelize this people group without requiring outside (crosscultural) assistance."[4]

The word *indigenous* is important here. The indigenous church or Christ group must be self-sufficient and thus can continue without outside support. Most important of all, a *reached* group can potentially have the local resources to maintain and expand its Christian population, even in highly restrictive environments such as those in which many of God's Special Envoys might work.[5]

The concept of a *Christ group* is used in this book to cover indigenous churches, as well as house churches and other secret gatherings of Christians that often must be the church alternatives in the restricted countries where Special Envoys will be sent.[6]

For our purposes, a *people* or *people group* is defined as a "grouping of individuals who perceive themselves as having a common affinity for one another" and who are made distinct from other groups by the combination of their language and ethnicity.[7] Examples of such distinct, ethnolinguistic groups include the Maasai tribes of Kenya or the Hmong hill tribes of Laos. According to an in-process document of the Adopt-A-People Clearinghouse, there are about 12,000 such *people groups* in the world today, of which 5,310 are still unreached. These 5,310 groups are referred to as either the *unreached peoples* or the *unreached people groups*. However, as the introduction of this document makes clear, many of the groups listed may actually be "groups of groups" or "clusters" such that the total could be twice as high as the 5,310 listed.

For the reader's convenience, appendix B provides a listing of the 145 countries in which these unreached peoples are located. Also included is the number of unreached peoples within each of these countries, plus the estimated numbers of non-Christians within each of these countries, as of 1995.

As can be seen from the Unreached Peoples Map, I have divided the 145 countries where the unreached peoples are located into six regions. The regions with lower numbers are gen-

Unreached Peoples Map

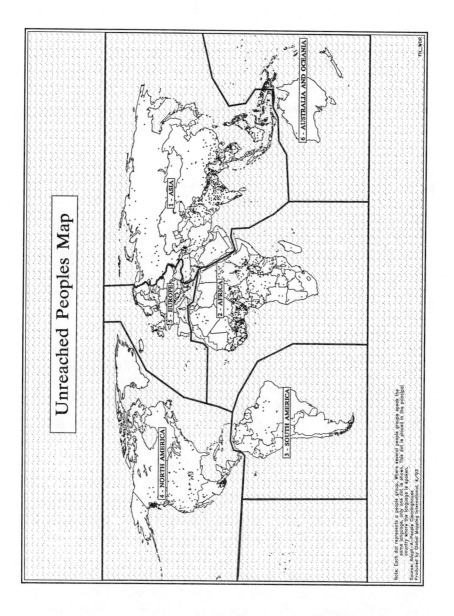

1 - ASIA

5 - EUROPE

2 - AFRICA

6 - AUSTRALIA AND OCEANIA

3 - SOUTH AMERICA

4 - NORTH AMERICA

Note: Each dot represents a people group. Where several people groups speak the
same language, only one dot is shown. This dot is placed in the principal
country where the language is spoken.

Source: Adopt-A-People Clearinghouse
Produced by Global Mapping International, 4/93

PPL_WOR

erally more afflicted by the combination of spiritual and physical hunger than those which have higher numbers. Individual maps of each of these six regions are also provided in appendix B.

Following each of the regional listings in appendix B, a total is provided for the estimated number of non-Christians (and people groups) within the specific countries within each of those regions. Adding up all of these regional totals indicates an estimated 3.88 billion non-Christians within the 145 countries that contain the 5,310 unreached people groups. This may give you some sense of the validity of this listing, which locates—at least by country—about 96 percent of all the non-Christians in the world in 1995.[8]

It is important to remember that this Adopt-A-People Clearinghouse listing is very new and is still considered a work-in-progress. It is presented here because it is one of the very best new tools we have available for targeting our mission efforts toward exactly those people groups that have been underserved by previous missionary efforts. The Adopt-A-People Clearinghouse and other mission researchers strongly suggest that anyone planning to work in a given people group verify in every possible way all the information relevant to that group prior to entering it. The results of such verification, as well as knowledge gained in the field, should also be fed back to the Clearinghouse, to refine its database for others.

In addition to the Unreached Peoples List and the Unreached Peoples Maps, there is another valuable aid for targeting the global evangelization effort. If you think of the Unreached Peoples List as the whole target, you might conceptualize this next aiming aid as the center portion, or "bull's-eye," of the target.

This "bull's-eye" is the map and listing of the 10/40 window countries. As you can see from the map, the 10/40 window is a somewhat arbitrary belt between 10 and 40 degrees north of the equator, stretching from western Africa to Asia across the Middle East. The 10/40 window countries are only those which have a

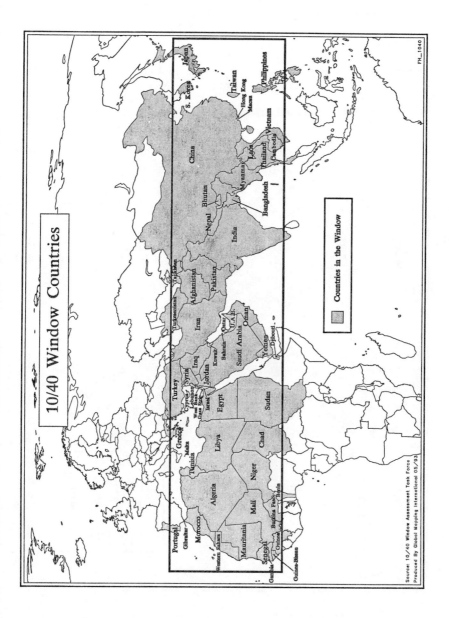

10/40 Window Countries

Countries in the Window

Source: 10/40 Window Assessment Task Force
Produced By Global Mapping International 05/93

FH_1040

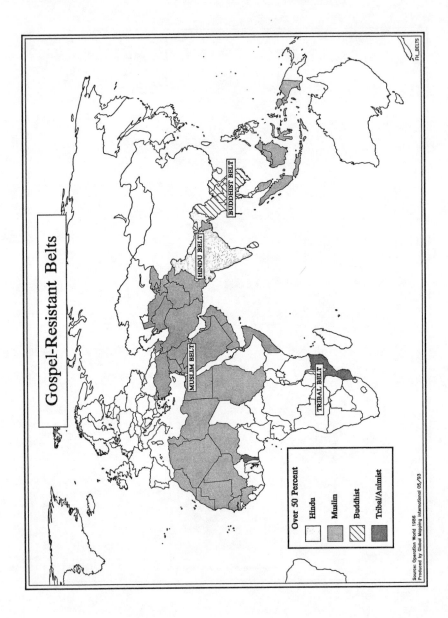

Gospel-Resistant Belts

BUDDHIST BELT

HINDU BELT

MUSLIM BELT

TRIBAL BELT

Over 50 Percent

Hindu

Muslim

Buddhist

Tribal/Animist

Source: Operation World 1986.
Produced by Global Mapping International 05/93

FN_BELTS

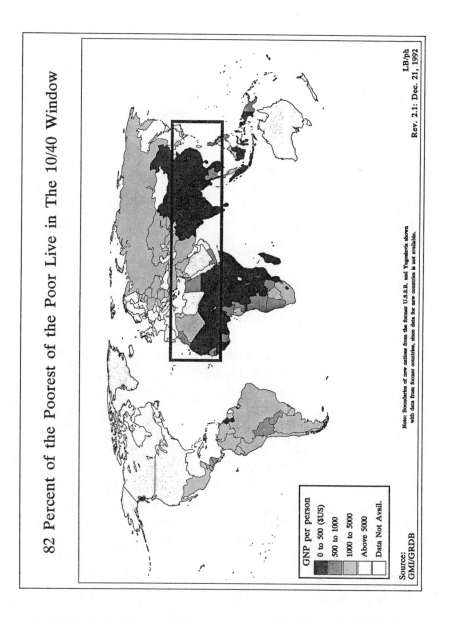

82 Percent of the Poorest of the Poor Live in The 10/40 Window

GNP per person (\$US)

0 to 500
500 to 1000
1000 to 5000
Above 5000
Data Not Avail.

Source:
GMI/GRDB

Note: Boundaries of new nations from the former U.S.S.R. and Yugoslavia shown with data from former countries, since data for new countries is not available.

LB/ph
Rev. 2.1: Dec. 21, 1992

majority of their land mass inside the belt. (They are all also countries with a population of at least five thousand.)[9]

The difference between the 145 countries on the Unreached Peoples List and the 59 countries in the 10/40 window is that whereas the countries in the first listing contain about 96 percent of the world's non-Christians, the shorter, "bull's-eye" list contains only about 79 percent of them. Nevertheless, the 10/40 window is a very valuable aiming tool.

To begin, this window contains practically all of the world's three largest gospel-resistant belts. As you can see, most of the Muslim world, the Hindu world and the Buddhist world are included within this window. And all three are prime targets for the new missionary strategy the Special Envoys can provide.

In addition, the 10/40 window includes twenty-three of the thirty countries (some 77 percent) that Barrett and Johnson identify as "unevangelized" (that is, "World A," their primary target for refocusing the mission effort).

Finally, the 10/40 window contains about 82 percent of the world's poor,[10] as well as eighteen of the world's forty least-developed countries.[11] Both of these attributes make the window especially relevant to the Special Envoys, whose specialty is the "two-hungers" ministry, aimed at people groups that are both unreached and suffering from physical needs.

In summing up these two targeting aids, my guess is that you may wish to use them both. Employ the list of 5,310 people groups when you want the full picture; use the 10/40 window when you want a narrower target on which to focus. Throughout all this, however, as the upcoming scriptural section will show, the focus on reaching unreached *people groups* is paramount (see Mt 24:14).

As Ralph Winter has said,

The use of "Unreached Peoples" (a non-geographical technology) is now making major changes in mission strategic thinking. . . . Mission does not mean going to *places* but to *peoples,* unreached peoples, to be precise—wherever representatives of such people are. . . . Missions is a specialized kind of evangelism, the kind which is a "first penetration" into a group which might otherwise never have a chance at all.[12]

Throughout this book the word *restricted* or *restricted-access* will be used to refer to people groups and countries that traditional missionaries—especially those with "MISSIONARY" stamped on their passport—will have difficulty entering. As of this writing Issachar provided a list of thirty-five of what they called "highly restricted" countries. Their rating is based on government restrictions on missionary visas, lack of constitutional freedom of religion, lack of *de facto* religious freedom and the like. Almost all of these countries are included among the unreached people group countries, and a great many of them are in the 10/40 window. I have decided not to reprint the list here, however, both because such lists change (for better or worse) very rapidly, and because there will be other kinds of restrictions on entering unreached people groups, even within countries that may not be seen as highly restricted.[13]

Another basic concept is *conversion*. As evangelicals we need to understand that what we mean—a spiritual transformation— is not what secular governments mean. In Matthew 28:19 Jesus says, "Go and make disciples of all nations, baptizing them in the name of the Father and of the Son and of the Holy Spirit." In other cases baptism is not mentioned, and the instructions are to accept the Lord Jesus Christ as Savior, possibly through a special prayer, public proclamation of faith, or some other means.

To avoid disputes about when precisely conversion takes place, I prefer a more global concept—that of *bringing people to faith and obedience in Christ* (Rom 16:26). This expression is quite precise and, it seems to me, describes our objective very well. The only problem, of course, is that it is measurable and quantifiable only in a practical and nonultimate sense. Thus, throughout this book I will sometimes be forced to quantify the concept of conversion in less precise terms. In many statistical cases, for example, I will talk about "professing" Christians—thereby basing the number of Christians on the number of individuals who claim the title of Christian as their own.

Through the years we have struggled to find better ways to count Christians in comparison to the national or international population at large. I generally prefer to use the term *communicants* (adult church members). This category is less elastic than the term *communities,* which some denominations (Roman Catholics, for example) prefer, and which includes not only adult members of a given church but also their children, who certainly tend to be influenced by their parents' religious preference. However, by converting all our figures whenever possible to communicants, we avoid the error of attempting to compare incomparables.

This is probably a good time to make another distinction, necessitated by the fact that there are currently 23,500 distinct denominations, all claiming to be the best way to follow the Way of Christ.[14] With this broad range of sometimes competing denominations, I want to clarify that the goal of this book is to help bring more people—in more unreached people groups—to faith and obedience in Christ, not to bring them to any particular denomination or group of denominations within the body of Christ.

I am confident that once the new convert has moved to faith and obedience, she or he will be properly guided as is required by the greatest Teacher of all. (Perhaps the best recent example of this is the explosive growth of the church in China after the expulsion of the missionaries.)

This is not to say that I lack personal convictions about ways of worship and interpretations of God's Word. These matters are of vital concern to me, as they are to most Christians. The burden of this book, however, is to develop strategies that can help bring hundreds of millions more people to Christ—not to dispute about fine points of doctrine, however important, with those who are already believers.

Our goal is to build up the body of Christ and to expand his church, not to weaken it through additional factional squabbles at a time when the salvation of billions depends on our working as one. Together as his church, the body of all faithful believers, we are charged to pursue the church's mission: to proclaim Christ and bring all people possible to faith and obedience in him.

A final expression, which I use frequently, is *the two hungers.* Actually, this started as a term that we employ in our relief and development ministry. The two hungers is simply a shorthand way to talk about people groups that are doubly burdened—both by physical hunger and need and by the lack of salvation through Jesus Christ. The first of these hungers is relatively straightforward. It includes malnutrition, undernutrition and lack of safe drinking water. Typically, it is also accompanied by lack of a reasonable level of health.

The second hunger—dealing with the spiritual—is more complex. As has been pointed out, and appropriately so, people in possession of a religion other than Christianity may not be aware that they are hungry at all.[15] Conversely, "hunger" in a spiritual sense may actually be a sign of spiritual health. This theme of healthy spiritual hunger—the desire to be in deeper union with God—is found throughout the Bible. Some wonderful examples include:

As the deer pants for streams of water, so my soul pants for you, O God. (Ps 42:1-2)

O God, you are my God, earnestly I seek you; my soul thirsts for you, my body longs for you, in a dry and weary land where there is no water. (Ps 63:1)

Blessed are those who hunger and thirst for righteousness, for they will be filled. (Mt 5:6)

There are also a number of other examples of this healthy spiritual hunger—a hunger that draws one closer to God. (See, for example, Ps 143:6; Lk 6:21.) However, our goal, as always, is to bring as many as possible—whether or not they now know they are hungry—to the one who said, "I am the bread of life. He who comes to me will never go hungry, and he who believes in me will never be thirsty" (Jn 6:35).

Rationale for Evangelism Abroad
Now that the necessary definitions have been spelled out, it is time to take the next step: to explore why we should be so audacious, and often so self-sacrificing, as to leave the comfort and security of our homelands to pursue crosscultural evangelism.

Many of the reasons for this are very old. Others are quite new, necessitated in recent years by changes in populations and governments. Although I review these reasons primarily for an audience in the more developed world, it should be noted that most of them will also have relevance to the less-developed world, which is now expanding its own Christian mission outreach at a rapid rate.[16]

Here are eight basic reasons for continuing and expanding our crosscultural evangelism abroad—or, if you prefer, the *global mission.*

1. *Because Christ mandated the global mission*—in Acts 1:8, Mark 16:15 and Matthew 28:19-20. Elsewhere he reinforces these instructions in different words:

Come follow me . . . and I will make you fishers of men. (Mt 4:19)

The Christ will suffer and rise from the dead on the third day, and repentance and forgiveness of sins will be preached in his name *to all nations,* beginning at Jerusalem. (Lk 24:46-47, my italics)

I tell you, open your eyes and look at the fields! They are ripe for harvest. (Jn 4:35)

As the Father has sent me, I am sending you. (Jn 20:21)
And finally, the instructions to Peter:

Feed my lambs. . . . Take care of my sheep. . . . Feed my sheep. (Jn 21:15-17)

2. *Because our Lord appears to establish global evangelism as a*

precondition of his return. In Matthew 24:14 he says, "And this gospel of the kingdom will be preached in the whole world as a testimony to all nations, *and then the end will come.*" Later, in Revelation 5:9, the risen Lord Jesus is addressed as one who "purchased men for God from every tribe and language and people and nation."

3. *Because as Christians we have received a precious gift which must be shared as widely as possible.* Put simply, if we are called to share our food, our cloaks, our shelter—which are only temporal things—how much more should we be called to share our greatest gift, the faith that provides eternal life?

4. *Because every individual is important and every individual's spiritual hunger deserves to be met.* Clearly John 3:16 emphasizes this divine intent of universal access to salvation: "For God so loved the world that he gave his one and only Son, that whoever believes in him shall not perish but have eternal life."

As long as we are alive and have breath in our lungs, those of us who have already heard the good news must continue to expend a portion of that breath to witness, so more of God's children can be saved.

5. *Because if we don't win those of our global neighbors who hunger for change, other, less desirable forces will.* Increasingly we see human hunger and need providing an opening for evil forces to move in. To see this truth, we only need to look at the rapid expansion of fundamentalist Islam and New Age cults.

As I said earlier, spiritual hunger seems to be basic to the human condition. So once that hunger is aroused, or—more accurately—once a person is made aware of its existence, the need will be filled somehow, by whatever religion or ideology is most persuasively represented to the person who hungers. Conversely, if Christianity is not effectively represented in the area when that hunger is experienced, the opening may pass forever.

6. *Because Christianity's adversaries are increasingly ruthless.* For many residents of the developed, democratic world, it's hard to grasp the true evil of some of the alternatives to Christianity—

religions and quasi religions that also vie for uncommitted hearts and souls. For some parts of the world, this alternative "religion" is still Communism. Elsewhere it may be voodoo or religions that subject adherents to drastic forms of sexual discrimination and physical abuse.

In recent years, the wanton murder of hundreds of thousands of Christians in Uganda by Idi Amin and the systematic torture and cruel imprisonment of the faithful in Vietnam under the guise of "reeducation" show the steps hostile governments are willing to take, regardless of world public opinion.

7. *Because only changed lives can change society, and only a changed global society can truly live in peace.* This is a personal favorite of mine, because it relates to my conviction, since my conversion almost four decades ago, that we can achieve "horizontal" peace in the world only as we increasingly, one by one, achieve "vertical" peace with God. On a practical level, there is surely no doubt that some of Christianity's strongest global competitors teach violence and strife: militant, fundamentalist Islam, dictatorial Communism, anarchism and, of course, the many quasi-religious forms of terrorism that permeate our world.

8. *Because Christian missionary work, in its many forms, is still one of the most satisfying adventures of all.* Never doubt the sheer excitement of working in foreign countries to help others find salvation.

These then are the eight reasons, any of which would be sufficient justification for pursuing global evangelization through financial support, through prayers and through service abroad.

To summarize, we need to reach out forcefully to the world's 5,310 unreached peoples . . .

☐ because it's commanded biblically

☐ because we are called to care about these people and their salvation

☐ because if we delay, billions of non-Christians may lose both their chance of eternal salvation and their opportunities for more satisfying lives right now

These then are some of the reasons all Christians should support the most vigorous possible evangelization effort to all the unreached peoples.

Next question: What kind of progress are we making toward that goal?

Questions for Thought and Review

1. What's the difference between "unevangelized" people and "unreached" people?

2. How would you characterize the people groups living within the 10/40 window?

3. Give five reasons why you feel global evangelism is required.

2
The Urgency of Missions' Final Frontier

On THE POSITIVE SIDE OF THE GLOBAL MISSION MOVEMENT, there are a lot of new tools available to assist missionaries with their work. These include the excellent new data resource of the Unreached Peoples List and Unreached Peoples Maps. These were previewed in the preceding chapter, and their creators anticipate that they will gain considerably in accuracy as they gain exposure and are updated with more input from the field.

There are also some other powerful new knowledge sources. Among these are David Barrett and Todd Johnson's *AD 2000 Global Monitor* trio. This includes a book, a user-friendly database and a newsletter—all representing "a serious attempt to *monitor* everything at the global level which is going on and which is relevant to world evangelization."[1]

The Peoples Information Network (PIN) collects and disseminates information about specific unreached people groups.

Additionally, there is a wide range of other mission aids, including the always popular *JESUS* film. This two-hour film is based on Luke's account of the life of Christ. It is now available in 241 different languages, with 100 more translations in progress and specialized equipment available for showing the film in remote regions.[2]

Added to these informational resources is a proliferation of new global evangelization plans. They seem to be emerging especially rapidly as the century draws to a close. At mid 1990, Barrett and Johnson estimated that there were "410 current global plans, with 260 current global plans making progress."[3]

That's the overview of some of the data resources, soul-winning tools and evangelization plans. But what about the results?

Performance in the Field Not Keeping Up

The honest truth is that in spite of these new and excellent resources—many the result of years of hard work—the gap between where we should be going and where we actually are continues to grow. Without a serious change in mission priorities, staffing and strategy, it would appear that our evangelization efforts to date will not be able to respond to the new factors and circumstances that confront us today. By mid 1995, as already discussed, we will almost certainly set a new record for those who live and die without Christ. In that year, a staggering four billion souls will be looking forward to an eternity of despair.

A number of factors account for these unpromising results, in spite of some hard-working mission professionals and a range of wonderful new knowledge and tools. A large force in the growth of the non-Christian world is simply that, in the aggregate, the non-Christian lands are generally experiencing a higher population growth rate than the countries that are already predominantly Christian. There are lots of exceptions to this trend, of course, but overall it holds up. The miracle is that the relatively small new evangelical populations in Africa, Latin America and Asia are growing so fast that they are more than making up for the massive slowdown of general population growth in the largely Christian West. The figure on page 45 shows this overall trend, depicting how the non-Christian growth is steadily and surely falling behind in its percentage of the world total.

There is also a serious lack of translations of Scripture, especially for the types of small people groups that comprise missions' final frontier. As of this writing, 4,980 languages have no scriptural translations yet. This is "a staggering challenge to global Christianity, since native speakers of these languages in 1993 numbered some 180 million. This leaves 180 million persons—3.1 percent of the world—with no access to the Scriptures in their mother tongue."[4]

Another factor inhibiting the global mission—one that was discussed in the introduction—is the inappropriate targeting of our mission priorities, with 99.9 percent of the Christian world's mission resources going to countries that are already Christian. This leaves only a tenth of a percent of these resources for the unreached people groups.[5]

Also in the introduction I discussed two other factors inhibiting our global mission results. The first is the lack of mission specialists who are trained to penetrate people groups that are highly resistant to the gospel and/or where the quality of life is exceptionally low. The second is the lack of a strategy to aid these new mission specialists in penetrating highly resistant and/or highly needy groups.

To summarize to this point, we need to evangelize faster and more effectively, just to keep up with the non-Christian population growth. But we cannot do so because we are spending our resources on the already converted and we lack the specialized personnel, specialized training and specialized strategy to evangelize in groups that either have not heard the gospel before or have heard it and have grown increasingly resistant to its message.

Another reason for urgency in developing a new strategy and new specialist mission personnel is that the gospel resistance in

Christian vs. Non-Christian Growth, 1900-2100

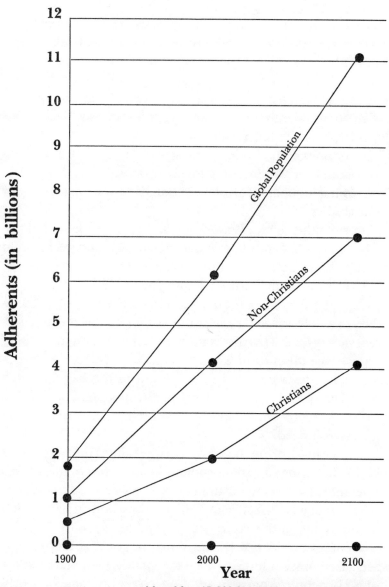

Adapted from AD 200 Global Monitor, No. 30, April 1993.
Source: World Evangelization Database

some of the world's largest non-Christian religions seems to be growing more intense. The case of the Muslims is especially critical, since more of the world's 935 million Muslims—about 18 percent of all humanity—are unreached. The opportunity here, as expressed by noted Islamic strategist J. Christy Wilson Jr., is enormous.

Muslims today are more open to the gospel than ever, Wilson says. "In the next ten years I see a great influx of Muslims to Christ if Christians take the Great Commission seriously." Wilson reports these heartening results:

☐ In Indonesia, the world's largest Muslim country, hundreds of thousands of Muslims have turned to Christ.

☐ Growing numbers of Muslims in Bangladesh are gathering for Bible studies.

On the other hand, Wilson notes, the consequences of not meeting this challenge to evangelize in the Muslim world could be dire: "If we don't go to the Muslims with the gospel of love, God will bring them against us in judgment. Muslim eschatology teaches that they will conquer the earth. They consider themselves in a holy war to take over the world." So the choices are a great victory for the Lord or continued violence for humankind.[6]

As we face the current mission context, with all of its urgency and challenges, we should take comfort in the fact that even though the growth curve of Christianity in general is flat, the growth curve of our fellow Bible-believing Christians is very impressive indeed.

As you can see from the accompanying chart, the percentage of Bible-believing Christians compared to the rest of the world's population has increased dramatically. In fact, Ralph Winter points out that Bible-believing Christians are now an astonishing one out of ten in the world population.[7] Surely, with odds like these, we can afford to field a much larger and increasingly specialized mission force to meet the challenge of reaching the last 5,310 people groups. In addition, Great Commission Christians have now reached a global total of 616 million;[8] again, a

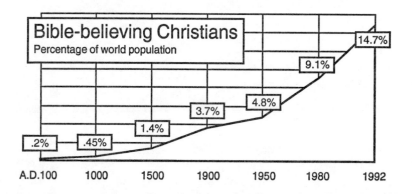

Bible-believing Christians
Percentage of world population

14.7%
9.1%
4.8%
3.7%
1.4%
.2% .45%

A.D.100 1000 1500 1900 1950 1980 1992

very abundant pool to draw from to field the large mission force that the present mission context requires.

As we face the challenge of penetrating missions' final frontier (that is, reaching the last of the unreached people groups), we have another advantage—perhaps the largest ever mobilization of truly focused prayer. By October 1993, it is expected that some thirty million Christians will be "praying through the window," praying that the unreached in the 10/40 window will finally come to a saving knowledge of Christ.

And as we face the specter of four billion persons who live and die without knowing Christ, we should pray as well. Therefore we turn to the Lord with prayers that he will guide his people in this work, as we resolve to do more in the great unfinished task.

Questions for Thought and Review
1. What does the author mean by "missions' final frontier"?
2. What are some of the factors that inhibit the global mission?
3. In comparison to the growth of the general population, has Christianity been growing numerically?

PART 2
God's
Special Envoys
Introduced

3
God's Special Envoys and Their Mission

SO FAR WE HAVE EXPLORED (1) THE MANDATE FOR THE GLOBAL mission, (2) why the unfinished task of the Great Commission has grown both more hopeful and more challenging than ever before, and (3) the new context facing our mission outreach in the coming years. We have thus identified the needs, the problems and the opportunities. Now, we turn to an important element of the solution—God's Special Envoys.

Their Place in the Mission Field
In this and the next few chapters we'll be developing the concept of God's Special Envoys and discussing how they are to be selected and trained—or perhaps how they can recognize this identity which they already possess. First, however, it might be helpful to look at the Special Envoys in context, to see where they fit in the overall fabric of the global mission effort.

To begin with, we must understand that these Special Envoys are intended to supplement the efforts of traditional missionaries and not to replace them or diminish the resources that support them. In fact, I believe that to fulfill their portion of the mission mandate over the next several years, traditional missionaries will require an increased allocation of resources and will need to be fielded in larger numbers than before.

I also think that we will find it productive to refine and intensify the training of traditional missionaries. They will need stronger specialized skills to meet the considerable challenge of more effectively evangelizing non-Christians in the countries best suited to traditional missionary approaches.

Later we'll explore a new model for evaluating which people groups are best served by traditional missionaries and which are more effectively reached by the Special Envoys. We'll also clarify the distinctions between traditional missionaries and the Special Envoys in the areas of training, support modalities and operating styles. For the present, however, a generalized comparison of the five basic groups of soul-winners might be of help, along with a look at this new group—God's Special Envoys.

Within these five groups—representing several million Christians throughout the world—resides the entirety of the human force now at work to activate the world's nominal Christians and to bring to Christ four billion who are not Christians at all. The accompanying chart gives a general description of each group in this multinational force, beginning with the smallest and working up to the largest. As the chart shows, God's Special Envoys are both the newest and the smallest segment of the large group of Christians now devoting some or all of their lives to global evangelization. Notwithstanding their relatively small numbers, however, the Special Envoys have been given a disproportionately large mandate: to reach the unreached peoples who are generally unreachable through traditional missionary efforts.

Also it should be understood that although God's Special

The Church's Worldwide Evangelistic Work Force—Five Essential Groups

1. God's Special Envoys

For the most part, these will be self-starters, self-supporting and cross-discipline trained in a nonmission area. In most cases Special Envoys will need to be silent about their "missionary vocation."

Their mandate: To work in countries most resistant to traditional approaches—to penetrate unreached people groups—especially those high in both spiritual and physical needs.

Their training and strategic approach: Largely new.

Current strength: In the tens of thousands. The exact figure is hard to estimate since many who fulfill a Special Envoy role have not yet understood this as their identity. There are also no tabulations kept of these specialists. Typically their identity is known only to the Lord, to themselves and to a small group of friends.

Minimum number required: 600,000. Though this number may at first sound high, it represents only one out of every one thousand Great Commission Christians in the world.[1] It is also important to remember that God's Special Envoys are a multinational force, supplied by whichever country has easiest access to a given unreached people group.

2. Traditional Missionaries

These tend to be under centralized control, to be supported by others and to have most of their training in traditional mission areas. They usually can be open about their missionary calling.

Their mandate: To evangelize winnable populations or people groups within relatively "open" countries.

Their training and strategic approach: Traditional, but being upgraded.

Current strength: About 285,250, plus 38,000 (a figure which is growing rapidly) from Third World countries.[2]

Number currently required: Hundreds of thousands more.

3. Other Full-time Christian Workers

This group includes pastors and other full-time ministers who are actively involved in evangelization. Its members are supported by others and almost always operate under some form of authority—a church committee, governing board, bishop or the like. The nature of their ministry is almost always openly disclosed.

Their mandate: To activate nominal Christians, to support the further growth of those who are already involved, and to "evangelize" (often nominal Christians) within their own geographic or ecclesiastical areas.

continued

Their primary target: In many cases, the 1.87 billion who already are professing Christians.

Current strength: About four million worldwide.[3]

Number currently required: Difficult to estimate. Depends on laity's willingness to shoulder more of the burden of evangelism.

4. Evangelizing Christian Laity

A voluntary group. Self-supporting, nonregimented, with widely divergent levels of training and willingness to assist in furtherance of the Great Commission.

Their mandate: Interpreted differently by different denominations.

Their target: Whatever population each group member selects for evangelization.

Their training and strategic approach: Varies widely.

Current strength: Difficult to measure, although there are currently 616 million "Great Commission Christians" (Barrett and Johnson) who potentially qualify for this role.

Number currently required: Many millions more.

5. Global Prayer Warriors

A voluntary group that prays for the unreached.

Their mandate: To pray for unreached peoples, often targeting a specific group over a long period of time.

Their target: Whichever of the unreached peoples they select.

Their training and strategic approach: Varies widely.

Current strength: At various times during these last years of the twentieth century, up to thirty million Christians have selected individual spiritually hungry countries and are praying that their inhabitants will be led to Christ.

Number currently required: Millions more.

Envoys will be "tentmakers" as the term is popularly understood in Christian missions, they will be more than tentmakers. "Tentmaking" refers primarily to an economic factor: a missionary's being financially self-supporting. But God's Special Envoys will be distinguished from traditional missionaries by much more than the financial self-support that will generally—but not always—characterize them. They will also be distinguished by their specialized training and the more difficult mission targets they select. In short, God's Special Envoys will be *specialists* in every sense of the word.

The Special Challenges They Must Meet

To meet the urgent needs in contemporary missions and to accelerate the global mission effort, these relatively new workers in God's vineyard will need to be very special indeed. In the words that have inspired missionary efforts for centuries, "The harvest truly is great, but the laborers are few: pray ye therefore the Lord of the harvest, that he would send forth laborers into his harvest" (Lk 10:2 KJV).

We have prayed to the Lord of the harvest, and we will continue to pray. It is hoped that the Special Envoys will be a portion of the answer. If so, they will be what Paul describes as "Christ's ambassadors" (2 Cor 5:20), meaning the messengers of the gospel of reconciliation—reconciling men and women of all races, all tribes, all language groups and all nations to God in Christ. As an urgently needed new breed of crosscultural workers, God's Special Envoys will be the lead force in penetrating missions' final frontier—the last unreached people groups.

Working within their special domain of unreached people groups suffering from the two hungers, these Special Envoys will strive to make disciples, to disciple the nations, and, especially, to reach the unreached—beginning immediately and continuing until the job is done.

In contrast to the church growth movement's strategy of "winning the winnable now," the Special Envoys will take for their harvesting target the groups that typically have proved the least winnable and the hardest to reach. These are also the groups that yield the greatest dangers, the most frustrations and the lowest conversion rates.

Their Basic Qualifications

Like any other missionary, the Special Envoys must be wholeheartedly devoted to Christ and his mission on earth, believing in the availability of salvation only in and through Jesus Christ. Also, like any other missionary, God's Special Envoys must be physically sound, emotionally stable, socially aware, culturally sensitive, biblically literate and very strong in their prayer lives. In addition, they will need to be equipped with a special strategy. To achieve their challenging mandate in the face of major changes in the mission field, they will require additional and very special qualifications.

God's Special Envoys—Qualifications
To be truly effective God's Special Envoys must meet the following qualifications:

Selection criteria
1. Physically, emotionally and spiritually self-reliant—to a very high degree.
2. Adaptable.

Training
3. Alert to the emerging mission context.
4. Trained in meeting needs vital to the people group they seek to penetrate.
5. Trained in long-term and low-profile evangelistic skills.

Strategy
6. Equipped with broad new strategic thinking.
7. Prepared with a special strategy for responding to opportunities presented by need.

These qualifications can be condensed into three separate yet interrelated categories: selection criteria, training and strategy. We will look at these more closely in the coming chapters.

There will be much here that is new, and I hope some thoughts can be adapted to increase the effectiveness of traditional career missionaries and ministries at home as well.

Questions for Thought and Review
1. Explain the position of Special Envoys with respect to traditional missionaries, pastors and other full-time workers.
2. Using your own words, make a list of criteria for selecting Special Envoys.

4
What Qualifications They Require

God's SPECIAL ENVOYS MUST BE CALLED FROM DIVERSE sources. The regions from which they emerge will include the developing world as well as the First World. In fact, a Third World background may well increase their credibility within many target groups.

Sources for Special Envoys

As stated before, Special Envoys will be people who are cross-trained—both with a practical development skill needed by the unreached people group and with a missionary's heart and, it is hoped, the training as well. They will thus be: (1) precareer people, with ministerial/missionary training already or at least the inclination to be so trained; (2) midcareer people, with ministerial/missionary training or at least the inclination to be so trained; or (3) postcareer people, preferably with ministerial/missionary training or at least the inclination to be so trained.

Clearly, good prospects to become Special Envoys can be found within a wide variety of groups. For example, they may be found among current college students, on both the undergraduate and graduate levels—majoring in subject areas such as comparative religion, biblical studies, science, agriculture, animal husbandry, engineering, medicine, anthropology, sociology, teaching, international law, diplomacy, intercultural communications and international business.

The "perennial student"—a sometimes maligned category—may be specially chosen for the Special Envoy role. If such a person feels called to long-term study within an unreached people group,[1] he or she will have access to indigenous fellow students—a group that may be especially open to the gospel. In such cases, the Envoy/student also may be able to gain access to additional members of the local community by teaching English as a second language, or teaching some other needed skill. This international student/tentmaker role thus becomes a very powerful way of penetrating the unreached people group. Additionally, it makes the student an expert on that group, filled with rare information that can enable other Special Envoys to penetrate that group effectively.

Executives and professionals of all kinds also are potential prospects for Special Envoy training. So are pastors and traditional missionaries on furlough seeking a new challenge in their careers.

Men and women in the military, teachers, and people working in diplomatic posts already may have performed as Special Envoys in the restricted-access countries where many of the unreached peoples live. What remains to be accomplished by them, however, is to commit to the Special Envoy role, to seek the additional training they require, and to maintain or resume their presence in the unreached people group.[2] Not only chaplains serving in the military, but all Bible-believing Christians serving as soldiers and their families can be Special Envoys, at least during the period of their stay in an unreached people group. The important thing is that they share the gospel.

I will always remember that my own conversion was through the ministry of such a person, Chaplain Vernon Kullowatz (United States Air Force), and his family. When I lived in Nagoya, Japan, in the 1950s, I also met many soldiers who made friends with Japanese young people and shared their testimonies. There is something especially powerful about the witness of soldiers, known for their courage and strength, talking about the peace of God.

For some midcareer traditional missionaries, the role of the Special Envoy may be exactly the fresh challenge for which they are looking. Remember, however, that the working environment for the Special Envoy can be quite different from that for traditional missionaries. Even more important, the low-key, one-on-one discipling style required of the Special Envoy may prove frustrating to the traditional missionary, especially if he or she is accustomed to high levels of harvesting for the Lord.

In a similar vein, we must stress that the skills of a successful pastor or a successful traditional missionary are very special—and a glorious gift from God—and may not fit comfortably into the less flamboyant, though often more entrepreneurial, evangelism style the Special Envoy must employ.

Some current missionaries and evangelizing development workers already are functioning as Special Envoys, in every aspect except for the title. As valuable as their individual contributions might be, however, role switching within Christ's current army is not the intent of this book. Rather, I believe we must use the banner of God's Special Envoys to raise up a new army—mobilizing thousands of previously underutilized Christians, providing them their own challenging and rewarding opportunity for a lifetime of service to the Lord.

I hope this cause is persuasive enough to reach some of those who previously have held back from personal evangelism. Some of this group may have mistakenly assumed that it is wrong to attempt to change another's religion. If so, they themselves are wrong: first, because it is the height of righteousness to share one's most valuable possession—the knowledge of the Lord; second, because no human can change another's religion. The true conversion must always be conducted by the Lord himself.

Others who have resisted the call to take part in personal evangelism have done so because of the mistaken assumption that "all religions are equally good and equally loved by God," or perhaps some notion that the "true path" would involve some sort of harmonious and mutually tolerant mixture of all the religions in the world.

For a refutation of these two false positions—known technically as relativism and syncretism—we need merely to take a more careful look at Scripture.[3] Or, if we prefer, we might look at some of the "fruits" of the other religions (such as Islam) and quasi religions (such as Communism) that flourish when the cause of Christ is not adequately championed.

One reason we might hope for many to respond to the call to join the ranks of God's Special Envoys is a response to the longing that is innate, though not always recognized, in us all. This is the longing for reconciliation and closeness with God, a need that can be satisfied in part through devotion of greater portions of our time and talent to his service. For some, this longing will be experienced as "not being right with God." For others, it may be perceived as what might be called an "unmet altruistic imperative." By that I mean the inner conflicts resulting from not currently fulfilling one's calling to do good in service to others.

One possible source of Special Envoy candidates might be from among those who are frustrated at our apparent helplessness in bringing peace to this world. Christians among the highly motivated men and women who serve in the U.S. Peace Corps (or its equivalent in another country) will appreciate opportunities to work for peace through the one-on-one contact that comes through serving as a Special Envoy. Christians who have completed their military obligation will also be sensitive to the important role Special Envoys can play in bringing lasting peace. As incidents of ethnic strife and civil wars multiply, many will be attracted by the Special Envoy's opportunity to make a lasting contribution to a better, more peaceful world.

Increasingly, the world's unreached peoples find themselves captivated by "religions" of violence. Within one group, the violence is practiced against women (in forms of Islam and animism). Within another, nonbelievers must die (in Islamic "Holy Wars"). In a third, the potential victims are a whole ethnic group, as in the "ethnic cleansing" that various groups practice against the weaker ethnic groups that live among them.

People in these unreached groups are also the victims of Western materialism, which has robbed them of resources that should be theirs. And we are all potential victims of environmental destruction, which degrades our sacred trust, the earth.

It would be an exaggeration, of course, to say that the Special Envoys can bring an end to all of this violence. Most assuredly, only the Lord Jesus has that power. But those who become Envoys will know that they are standing up against violence in a highly moral and caring way, and that each new individual they help bring to Christ will increase the total of our fellow human beings who can live in an eternal paradise of peace.

Being a Special Envoy should also appeal to those who want a firsthand experience within another culture. It is an ideal way to share profoundly close and satisfying human fellowship across cultural lines.

In addition, the role of Special Envoy should resonate for those who wish to affirm the most basic of human freedoms: the freedom of speech, the freedom of information, the freedom of choice. As God's Special Envoys, they are putting their lives on the line to fight for the right of unreached peoples to enjoy these rights, which most of us have learned to take for granted. More specifically, the Special Envoys will go forth not only under the

banner of Christ, though this would be enough. They march also
under the banner of the Universal Declaration of Human Rights,
Article 18. This says, and their actions help to ensure, that:

> everyone has the right to freedom of thought, conscience and
> religion; this right includes freedom to change his religion or
> belief, and freedom, either alone or in community with others
> and in public or in private, to manifest his religion or belief
> in teaching, practice, worship and observance.[4]

In summary, being one of God's Special Envoys is an excellent
vocation for Bible-believing Christians who care, who want to
learn, who will work to extend "universal" freedoms, and who
want to spread the kingdom of God.

Selection Criteria

The most basic criteria for selecting Special Envoys are that they
want to serve and that they seem to have the capacity for service
under the particular circumstances of restriction, aloneness and
potential danger. With so many available avenues for service to
the Lord, it is important that God's Special Envoys be the people
who are best suited for this task.

One essential component for the Envoys, in my opinion, is a
sense of wonder: a genuine desire to be immersed in a complex
foreign culture and to learn as much as possible about how it
works. This sense of wonder is not dissimilar to the thought
expressed in Paul's prayer for comprehension in Ephesians 3:

> And I pray that you, being rooted and established in love, may
> have power, together with all the saints, to grasp how wide and
> long and high and deep is the love of Christ, and to know this
> love that surpasses knowledge—that you may be filled to the
> measure of all the fullness of God. (Eph 3:17-19)

Granted, as we study a foreign culture we are not directly studying God; but in a sense we are. For can we not learn of the Father
by learning about his children, whom he created and loves so
much? More important, what better way is there to know our
Master than to walk with him, doing the work that he himself

did, and that he instructed us to continue in his name? With a true willingness to learn, the Envoys' days will be filled with new knowledge, and they will be more trusted by the people they seek to evangelize.

The Special Envoy also must develop the capacity to see "foreigners" as God does. Borrowing from Gordon Aeschliman and Sam Wilson's colorful expression, the Special Envoy must be able to understand that "God loves a Muslim as much as he does Billy Graham. We have to let go of prejudices and fears and see all people as precious."[5]

Elsewhere, Aeschliman echoes a similar theme. Though his comments address missions to the former Soviet Union, they can be applied to the residents of any country whose government is seen as hostile to the Envoy's native land.

But what about when we do recognize evil in their society? God requires us to respond by seeking ways to love them. . . . We must learn to love the Russians with the same tenderness that Jesus has for us, and that he has for the Russians.[6]

Another side of this ability to love—or possibly its result—is a willingness to go to corrupt countries, to dirty countries, even to sinful countries. The Special Envoy must have the sincere willingness to go wherever necessary and to do whatever is required to bring the unreached to Christ.

Obviously this kind of service demands that the Envoy be more than usually healthy and physically resilient. A physical constitution that requires frequent medical tune-ups would be a great handicap in most unreached areas, where medical assistance is often days away.

In one of my recent visits to our field staff in East Africa, I joked with a veteran missionary that driving skills on ravaged roads should be taught in all mission schools. We both laughed, but I'm not sure I was wrong. Perhaps one can learn the driving skills in-country, but one should certainly arrive there with a body resilient enough to take the strain.

Also on the subject of missionaries and strain, conventional wisdom in missionary selection would seem to indicate that there is less wear and tear on missionaries in isolated regions if the missionary is accompanied by a spouse. In the case of Special Envoys, however, I'm not sure that having a spouse is always required, or is even desirable in some situations. First, there is an element of physical danger in some of the more restricted areas. In such cases, as under a severe totalitarian regime, I suspect that single Envoys might feel less vulnerable than those who had an in-country spouse who was also liable to arrest. Individual situations vary, but there are also many crosscultural situations where a lone Envoy would become acculturated faster than one buffered by a spouse and maybe children as well. The point is, there are no simple rules. Certainly an unmarried Envoy should not resist going into an otherwise appropriate mission area simply for lack of a spouse.

Adaptability is another requisite for Special Envoys. They must be able to make the most of whatever opportunities the Lord brings them. Likewise, they must be flexible enough to let go of situations that are not turning out. In such cases, if people will not welcome them and listen to their words, they must be prepared to "shake the dust off [their] feet" and move on (Mt 10:14).

Like the desert fathers of the fourth century, the Special Envoys must be people who have cultivated great patience. To prevail, especially in some of the more bureaucratic and restrictive regimes, they often will have to sit and listen and wait.

Similarly, they must be able to find satisfaction in small results. Many times they will have to make do with a tiny mustard seed of a conversion and with a flowering of their efforts that may hardly be visible to them at all. They must always be humble enough to remember that though they are the ones who plant and water, "only God . . . makes things grow" (1 Cor 3:7).

The Special Envoy will also need to be proficient at a ministry of igniting others. He or she must be a teacher, an inspirer, a model for others. Special Envoys must demonstrate their beliefs through their own example. They must be able to work through the local structure and empower those who will be left behind after they leave.

Ray Giles, former codirector of personnel for the Christian Missionary Fellowship, has had a long missionary career in some especially difficult fields, including service in capacities where he was unquestionably one of God's Special Envoys. In one report on his research, Ray outlined three important indicators of eventual success in difficult mission fields:

The most significant factor is one's relationship to Jesus Christ. . . . A missionary must be content with his or her position in Jesus Christ and be able to sustain that relationship through prayer and meditation on the Word without the usual props and promptings of the church.

Second . . . is a healthy self-esteem. By that I mean one that does not run roughshod over colleagues or demand center stage. Even more dangerous is a low self-esteem, because there is little on the field to boost self-esteem.

A third factor has to do with mood-swings, especially those that shift to depression frequently. Successful candidates (the research indicates) . . . were rated by their acquaintances as rarely experiencing moodiness.[7]

The Three Pillars of Spiritual Support

Building on Ray's observations—which I heartily endorse—I think a little more needs to be said about the Special Envoys' foundation of spiritual strength. Especially important are three pillars of their support: the Lord's presence, Scripture and unity with other believers.

Even in sometimes desperately lonely places, the Envoys will never be alone. They will be aided in all their trials by the constraining love of Christ and by the Great Comforter, the Holy Spirit.

Not having "the usual props and promptings of the church," however, they will probably need to turn to Scripture with greater regularity, certainly on a daily basis. Scripture will also be the common philosophical basis for all the Envoys, ensuring that they are "thoroughly equipped for every good work" (2 Tim 3:17).

Along with the love of Christ, Scripture will be the transcendent commonality that empowers Special Envoys to work together as one—though separated by enormous distances, being without central leadership, and coming from diverse backgrounds and nations—to achieve the overarching goal of the Great Commission.

An additional important selection criterion for Special Envoys is their ability to work in harmony as members of diverse groups of committed Christians, where differences in background and training will produce differences in doctrine and approach.

In part, this unity of the Special Envoys will be achieved automatically by the severity of the mission field. This can be attested by most anyone who has experienced mission efforts in some of the extremely hostile nations where Special Envoys will be called to work. In part, this ability to work together must be taught.

Don Hamilton, director of TMQ Research, conducted a survey of 349 tentmaker missionaries working overseas. The responses of the 16 percent of those surveyed who were found to be most effective in the field were then analyzed, and some common characteristics were identified. Here are five of the characteristics identified by the Hamilton survey, along with Don's comments about them. All five, in my opinion, will also prove to be important indicators of the effectiveness of God's Special Envoys.

1. *They had led an evangelistic Bible study before going overseas.*

It is felt that this is significant because conventional witnessing methods, such as door-to-door visitation, passing out tracts, holding street meetings, etc. are not wise or even possible in many places in the world. Building relationships, earning the right to be heard are key. An evangelistic Bible study is a fine strategy.

2. Their main reason for going was to share the gospel of Christ.
Travel, money or desire to be independent were not strong
motivating factors. Without motivation to share the gospel,
less effective tentmakers quickly burn out in the often hostile
environments.

3. They believed that God called them to be tentmakers.
When the going got tough, many indicated it was their deep
conviction of God's calling that carried them through. The
emphasis was on absolute assurance that this is where God
wanted them.

4. They had experience in actively sharing their faith at home.
Their expression was that "if you hadn't done it here, you
wouldn't there, where it is 100 times tougher." As compared
to the "average" tentmaker, twice as many of these highly
effective tentmakers witnessed about Christ overseas, and
three times as many led others to Christ while there.

5. They had strong relationships with their home local church.
Their attendance and participation were consistent, and their
church considered their tentmaking work true missions activity. Most were commissioned by their church, and reported
back to and felt accountable to their church.[8]

Having discussed the selection processes for the Special Envoys,
the subject of the next chapter is their training.

Questions for Thought and Review

1. Explain where potential Special Envoys are to be found.
2. Describe what is so new and different about them.
3. Discuss your reactions to the three factors suggested by Ray Giles and
the findings of Don Hamilton's tentmaker effectiveness survey. How
relevant do you think these factors are to the effectiveness of Special
Envoys?

5
Special Training for the Challenge

In DESIGNING A TRAINING PROGRAM FOR GOD'S SPECIAL ENvoys, we need to create a curriculum for a group that has only recently been recognized, the goal of which is to do something that has rarely before been done. And I'd like to suggest even more hurdles that must be cleared.

First, this training needs to be widely available. It should attract both college and graduate students from all over the Christian world, and yet also appeal to more mature candidates who already are in midcareer, offering them training—or re-training—that provides the least possible interruption of their current careers and their lives.

Second, this training needs to be interesting and challenging enough that bright, resourceful and well-educated people will be attracted. Our goal is to attract people who are already successful—whether in a school setting or in a career. The mission of God's Special Envoys is difficult and demanding. Only superior candidates need apply.

Third, this training needs to provide—or strengthen—a skill that is seen as both relevant and *necessary* to the people group where the Envoy will serve. Such skill, or profession, must be a good fit within a group about which, in some cases, little may be known.

Fourth, this training needs to be built on an unquestionably sound biblical base, so that candidates from the broadest possible range of Christian denominations will be comfortable with it. As stated earlier, the Special Envoys are seen as a bridge to span the rifts caused by denominational rivalries. Nothing less than a unified body working together can achieve the Great Commission; nor, as Christians, should we accept anything less than a truly united attempt.

Today's Mission Context

Earlier we described the "mission context" at the end of the twentieth century. Naturally, in order for Special Envoy training to be relevant, it must include instruction that will enable Envoys to evangelize effectively in the midst of these new environments. Depending on the country or people group where they will be working, God's Special Envoys must be prepared to face any or all of the following nine elements:

1. the exploding non-Christian population
2. the persistent restrictiveness of the remaining people groups that still haven't heard the gospel
3. the problems of reaching across cultural barriers and being believed, trusted and understood
4. the shift of the church's population centrum from the developed West to the Third World
5. the growing eagerness of Third World Christians to have a substantial role in the mission effort
6. the need for church planting strategies to fit countries where Christians may receive no outside support
7. the shift of the church's membership base from the church

of the haves to "the church of the poor"

8. the high incidence of physical need within unreached people groups

9. the ambition of the leadership of many of these unreached groups to "catch up" with the prosperity and power of the developed world

From a review of these nine aspects of the emerging mission context, we can develop specific performance objectives for Special Envoy training. These are not intended to indicate all the things a Special Envoy should know related to the current mission context, but they will suggest some of the kinds of knowledge required.

Following their training, Special Envoys should be able to:

1. List and explain the strategy and tactics for penetrating (that is, evangelizing and converting within) the people groups where there is a high level of need.

2. Identify the techniques for entering people groups most resistant to the gospel.

3. Explain and demonstrate techniques for communicating successfully with people from a different culture—paying special attention to dissimilar values, ethnocentricity, nonverbal communication (such as proxemics and gaze behaviors) and the culturally value-laden conversion issues such as polygamy or alcohol consumption.

4. Demonstrate a sound knowledge of the Third World—its strengths and weaknesses. Describe the more common Third World social systems and hierarchical structures. Explain the rationale for working "under" Third World nationals.

5. Describe five or more church-planting tactics designed for countries where traditional churches are not tolerated. Explain and differentiate the techniques for discipling, "friendship evangelization," "relationship evangelization" and building up self-replicating Christ groups.

6. Explain basic techniques for winning another person to Christ, especially when that person is a member of a cultural

group different from your own. Be able to demonstrate these techniques in practice. Also, demonstrate actual experience utilizing these techniques with various ethnic groups under controlled, supervised circumstances where your approach can be critiqued and improved.

7. Explain and demonstrate, in actual practice, techniques for organizing and perpetuating a Christ group. Participate in this group both as leader and member.

8. Explain techniques for teaching local nationals to take up the missionary task, working independently of you, without any outside support.

9. Develop and explain a personally comfortable rationale for operating as a "covert" missionary whose official and public status is other than Special Envoy.

10. Demonstrate acceptable mastery of whatever language will be required in your mission field. (Note: Depending on the situation, some of this mastery might have to be acquired after entering the field.)

11. List and explain the basic tenets of the dominant religions and quasi religions (such as Communism) within your selected mission field. List ten strengths of these religions and ten ways in which Christianity might better meet the local population's needs.

At all phases of their training, it is vital that the Envoys learn attitudes that are culturally nonjudgmental. They must be taught that they are not going abroad to make *American* Christians or *Japanese* Christians or *French* Christians or *Belgian* Christians. Rather, they must strive to bring unreached peoples to faith and obedience in Christ, so these peoples can then be Christians in a way that is both biblically sound and authentic within their indigenous cultural systems.

It is also imperative that all training place a high priority on quality—quality of preparation, quality of personal example and quality of sharing with those whom you seek to bring to faith and obedience in Christ.

The expectation of the Special Envoys is not that they will immediately—if ever—be able to lead large numbers of people to Christ, and certainly not in a brief period of time. It is assumed that in the areas where Special Envoys will work, the conversion process will take a great deal of time, discretion, skill, patience and prayer.

Some, if not many, of the unreached groups where Envoys will work have already been evangelized, at least to a degree. The problem is that this evangelization has not "taken." The population or its government is just too resistive, and no indigenous churches have sprung up. The solution to this resistiveness requires Envoys who will set a truly inspiring example of Christian conduct, and who must be equipped with the special skill of teaching disciples who can teach other disciples, who will then together be able to create an indigenous church.

Thus, God's Special Envoys need to be effective one-on-one teachers. They must have the skills to raise up disciples who can work independently as persuasive witnesses for Christ. We need to look no further than the apostle Paul to understand the critical importance of a single convert who has the credentials to be persuasive to those within his own culture, and who has been properly inspired and taught. The special mission of the Special Envoy is one in which the greatest successes will probably be achieved by those whom the Envoy disciples, rather than by the Envoy.

Special Disciplines

Obviously, each Envoy's training will vary, depending on where he or she goes to seek that training, and the degree to which such training takes place in the classroom or is acquired on the job or through independent study. In any case, the following will provide a general outline for the components and the disciplines that the Envoys' training should include:

1. *Biblical/theological studies.* Includes at least a year of scriptural studies and Christian apologetics to thoroughly prepare the Envoy to use the Bible as a tool—both for evangelization and for

personal daily guidance and sustenance.

2. *Crosscultural training.* Includes language learning, traditional religions, cultural adjustment, issues in crosscultural communication, social structure (authority patterns), crosscultural exposure and so on.

3. *Missiology.* Includes history of mission, theory of mission, church growth case studies, theory and practice of symbiotic ministries, and so on.

4. *Development issues and global awareness.* Includes issues related to the relief-recovery-development-sustainability continuum; economic, social and political considerations affecting developing nations; world hunger and the politics of hunger; and so on.

5. *Spiritual growth.* Includes spiritual development prior to the beginning of the Special Envoy's ministry and also spiritual training to keep that ministry Christ-centered and Spirit-filled.

6. *Passport skills.* Includes specialization in an area such as agriculture, education (for example, teaching English, German, Japanese and so forth as a second language), suitable technology, health, nutrition, management or internship with an international development agency.

If the prospective Special Envoy is still in a formal academic environment and can afford the time, a variety of disciplines might prove highly fruitful as background for Special Envoy training: cultural anthropology, applied anthropology, comparative religion, sociology (with respect to group dynamics), world history, intercultural communication, world religions, and areas of engineering and agroscience that would enable the Special Envoy to develop skills useful in a Third World setting.

It is assumed that the Special Envoys' training will include both formal and nonformal education. Typically the formal education will be part of a degree program and will be credential-based. It will tend to be more preparatory in nature and require full-time learning. It will take place in an institution, with a teacher and preestablished standards of performance.

The nonformal portion of the education, on the other hand, will be more short term and specific, and take place part time. It will be more practical and will more likely be customized to the specific needs of the Envoy in the specific situations he or she expects to meet. This nonformal education will probably take place in the community, possibly within a setting where the Envoy is receiving practice in some of the skills required in the field (for example, working in an ethnic ministry in an urban setting). Quite possibly the Envoy will establish the performance criteria for this nonformal education and will be responsible for determining at what point the education has been a "success."

If the Envoy is to work in a context of need, he or she will require additional areas of training. The amount of time spent on these areas will, of course, depend on the specific kinds of work the Envoy will undertake in the target group. For Envoys concerned with development and human need, we recommend training in the principles of relief and development, project management techniques, theory and methods of mental and physical growth, and public health techniques.

A number of Christian relief and development organizations, such as Food for the Hungry, offer well-supervised field internship programs that could provide a prospective Special Envoy with outstanding experience both in relief and development work and in Christian witness within a gospel-resistant country. In many cases, these programs do not require extensive prior experience. One must meet three main criteria for acceptance: (1) a desire to serve in a Third World setting in Christ's name, (2) a willingness to learn the necessary relief and development skills, and (3) the ability to make a commitment of two to three years to this work.

By now it should be apparent that embedded within the Special Envoy training are many of the basic components of traditional missionary instruction. Time permitting, it would certainly be appropriate for the Special Envoy to complete all the traditional missionary basic training, in addition to the specific skills required in the Special Envoy context.

Practically, what this means is that a traditional missionary may well be attracted by the Special Envoy field and seek to acquire the Special Envoy training at midcareer. Traditionally trained missionaries who already have solid experience in some of the more restrictive mission fields would be ideal candidates to become Special Envoys, and might find that the change would add new challenge and enrichment to their vocations.

In addition, the Envoys should also have training in ways to maintain their physical and psychological health, and a clear understanding of the extreme physical, psychological and spiritual pressures they may experience.

As mentioned previously, before they travel to their mission field, it is highly desirable that the Special Envoys have already demonstrated strong one-on-one evangelization skills. One excellent and productive way to hone these skills might be in a ministry to foreign students in the educational institution where Envoys gain some of their training. This means of evangelism training has special benefits, in addition to the conversions achieved. It gives the Envoy candidate experience working with a foreign population, and because of the selection process by which usually only the elite may study abroad, the Envoy might reach future leaders who, in turn, could improve the climate for the Christian missionaries in their homelands.[1]

A related, but more humble, way to begin the process is for the Envoy-in-training to request to be included in a worship group conducted by Christian students from another culture. In this way the prospective Envoy will learn that there are many authentic ways to practice true Bible-believing Christianity. In addition, he or she might also experience the special energy that accompanies Christian worship in groups where the decision to follow Christ sometimes leads to martyrdom.

The Passport Skill
The degree to which Special Envoys can be trained to cope with

the current mission context will determine the degree to which they can succeed in achieving their mandate. One basic step in this direction is the expectation that all Envoys be trained both in the specialized mission skills that they will require (as described above) and also in a separate skill or professional area that will make them a "valuable commodity" for the population that they wish to reach.

Just as the name implies, this "passport" skill will be the skill or profession that appears on the Envoy's visa application and passport. Obviously, the skill must be attractive enough to motivate the host government to permit the Special Envoy to work in the country for a year or more.

Perhaps not quite so obviously, the passport skill must also give the Envoy access to the most likely candidates for evangelization within the target group. Within some countries, one might prefer a skill that would put the Envoy in contact with an agricultural population. In another situation, a scientific discipline or a manufacturing specialization might produce more productive access to a group most likely to be open to the gospel and to Christ.

The point is that the passport skill is the admission ticket to the mission theater. This skill (rather than the "missionary" vocation) will be the identifying label Envoys use in the mission context.

To an increasing degree, the areas of the world most restricted to missionaries tend also to be resistant to many forms of "foreign interference." Thus, the few foreigners who are permitted access to these areas are usually expected to have more than usual credentials. For example, a university teaching situation would probably require a Ph.D. In nursing, a registered nurse with a four-year degree and possibly additional certification might find admission to the host country and a strategically located placement more likely.

For gaining access to key individuals in the target group, an executive in a multinational corporation or an individual with highly prized scientific or industrial skills might be an excellent candidate to be a Special Envoy. In this case, the desirability to the host country of the Envoy's passport skill and the potential level of his or her contact in the host group might outweigh a possible lack of previous mission experience. Naturally the Envoy candidate would still need the special training described earlier, though much of this could be learned on his or her own. Such self-instruction would be less than ideal, but the chance to place an Envoy in a key position in the target group might well outweigh the disadvantages. If forced to design such an on-location program of study, the Envoy would have to trust more than usual in the guiding power of the Holy Spirit, the greatest teacher of all. In some unreached groups in particular, the Envoy would also have to be very cautious about importing Christian materials for the education process.

One fundamental point where Envoy careers will differ from the career criteria for traditional missionaries is that the Special Envoys will generally need to be self-supporting in the field. Likelihood of being a "tentmaker" (Acts 18:3) would, of course, give the Envoy less time for evangelizing. But it would also produce important benefits. First, the Envoy's mission activities would be untraceable, since there would be no sending body. Second, the Envoy's passport profession would create natural working opportunities for witness. And third, there would be no need to leave the mission field at regular intervals to secure funds. Being a tentmaker is also consistent with one of the basic premises of the Special Envoys: they should not compete for resources (that is, mission support) that current traditional missionaries require.

Depending on the needs and resources of the Envoy's target group, a wide variety of passport skills might be appropriate. One might teach English as a second language in China or in a Muslim country. A nurse or a doctor might work for an international health care agency and live in Afghanistan, Burkina Faso or Chad. The host government might seek qualified teachers in such areas as animal husbandry, water conservation or public health. A Western diplomat sent to a limited-access country in North Africa might have ample opportunities to hold regular Bible studies in his home. In a culture where cattle are important (as they are, for example, in India, Thailand or among Kenya's Maasai), a veterinarian might possess the right keys to open many doors (and hearts). A skilled relief professional will also be welcome in many situations—and may (as we will see later) experience some of the most fruitful evangelization opportunities of all. Almost any productive, peaceful and ethical skill that the target group is seeking could be a good passport skill for the Special Envoy.

And so, properly selected and cross-disciplinary trained, the Special Envoy would appear to be ready for the field. First, however, there is one additional piece of training, a new discipline to master: the strategy that will enable the Special Envoys to handle the enormous task ahead.

Questions for Thought and Review

1. In brief, what is the current emerging mission context that God's Special Envoys must face?

2. In your opinion, what are the most essential elements in the training of Special Envoys?

3. Explain the term "passport skill" and describe a passport skill you already have or might wish to acquire.

Part 3
The
New Missions'
Strategy

6
The Basic Strategy for Reaching the Unreached

Like MOST OF WHAT IS NEW, THE "NEW STRATEGY" FOR REACH-ing the unreached that I am now about to present is built upon the work of others. You will meet some of these mission pioneers in the pages that follow. However, let me give you the overview of this strategy—in its latest form—as it has evolved through my research and writing over nearly twenty years. In its most basic outline, the strategy can be summarized as three basic proposals.

First, I propose the identification, selection, training and mobilization of a new group of 600,000 mission specialists. They should be cross-trained in both development and missionary skills, though the latter area will be disclosed only selectively within the people groups where they work.

Second, I propose that these specialists—whom I call "God's Special Envoys"—concentrate their efforts exclusively on one of the 5,310 last unreached people groups that years of effort have finally allowed us to identify.[1] In particular, they should focus on one of the 4,000 or so of these groups in which physical needs are great.

Third, I propose that these Special Envoys are to *supplement* the efforts of traditional missionaries and the organizations that support them—efforts that also need to be increased. To avoid draining resources from these other essential efforts, God's Special Envoys are to generate their own support (as tentmakers) or to create new support mechanisms, none of which should interfere with the efforts of traditional missionaries.

As should be clear, this Special-Envoy, two-hungers strategy is designed as a supplementary strategy. As such, it should enhance (rather than conflict with) most of the plans for world evangelization that are appearing at an accelerating rate as the twentieth century draws to a close.[2]

In sending out this new force of 600,000 Special Envoys to penetrate the unreached people groups—where both physical and spiritual hungers are great—we send them into a life-or-death battle outnumbered about five thousand to one.[3] Equipped with their Bibles and God's love, they go up against some of the world's most restrictive governments, entering their most inaccessible lands, and facing some of their most devastating perils of physical torture and disease.

Obviously, they can succeed only with God's help, invoking the same claim that Paul made when he struggled to gain strength for his own overwhelming ministry some nineteen centuries ago:

But he [the Lord] said to me, "My grace is sufficient for you, for my power is made perfect in weakness." Therefore I will boast all the more gladly about my weaknesses, so that Christ's power may rest on me. That is why, for Christ's sake, I delight in weaknesses, in insults, in hardships, in persecutions, in difficulties. For when I am weak, then I am strong. (2 Cor 12:9-10)

Clearly, God's grace is sufficient. But we also need to be good stewards of the talents that he has given us. To this end, we must maximize the effectiveness of the 600,000 who face such overwhelming odds.

As with any battle, the outcome will be influenced by a number of factors. Two of these—superior personnel and superior training—have already been discussed. The third factor—a superior strategy—is the subject of this and the next two chapters.

The Nine Steps

To help develop and understand the overall strategy, we first need to see it within a broader context. To provide this, I begin with an overview of the nine steps that research shows we must take in order to reach the remaining unreached people groups. Though some would disagree, I believe that each of these steps must be taken for each of the groups, though our present coordinated mission efforts should allow us to pool our efforts in many of these steps.

Each of the nine steps is presented with a few comments to help you understand its role in the overall process of the human side of the efforts to bring a group from ignorance of the gospel to possession of a viable and indigenous church. Understanding this process, as Donald McGavran told us nearly forty years ago, is the key to answering "perhaps the most important question [in missions] of all—How do Peoples become Christian?"[4]

1. Vision. The first step is to have a vision by which this great work can be accomplished.

2. Identification. The second step is to identify by name, location and needs the unreached peoples who are the targets of this attempt.

As I have shown, these first steps have already been taken with the coming together of an increasingly unified global evangelization plan, focused on the last 5,310 people groups.

3. Prayer. With this third step, Christians pray in a focused and ongoing manner for the unreached groups.

4. Adoption. In the fourth step, individual Christians, individual churches and mission agencies adopt specific unreached people groups.

As of this writing, these steps are being taken through the tireless efforts of the Adopt-A-People Clearinghouse, the AD

2000 and Beyond Movement, and similar programs aimed at adoption and prayer. In regard to prayer, some thirty million Christians around the world focused their prayers on the "least evangelized" countries within the 10/40 window in a major effort that began in October 1993. Many of the individuals and groups that have already participated in this "Praying Through the Window" will no doubt continue to pray for their selected countries in the years ahead. Similarly, the efforts continue to have every one of the 5,310 unreached peoples adopted by churches and agencies that will focus their prayers and other resources on the establishment of an indigenous and viable church in each of those groups.

5. *Mobilization.* Within the framework of this book, step five is the mobilization of 600,000 Special Envoys, who will penetrate the four thousand or so unreached people groups in which physical need is extreme.

6. *Training.* Similarly, this step, as discussed in chapter five, specified the training this new force of development/missionary specialists will require.

7. *Engagement.* This seventh step is the focus of much of the rest of this present chapter. Engagement includes the specific tactics that the Special Envoys use to enter and begin establishing a viable, culturally indigenous church within the two-hungers people groups that they are called to penetrate.

As should be apparent, the thrust of the present book is to elaborate on these last three steps (five, six and seven), especially as they apply to effective evangelism through relief and development—the special task of the Special Envoys. The reader should also be aware that there are two more steps. These, like all the others, are also essential, though space permits only brief mention of them here.

8. *Assessment.* In this eighth step, agencies furthering the global mission must have the discipline to evaluate critically the actual results they achieve. This step is essential, as David Barrett[5] and others stress. Without honest and thorough assessments we

will never know if our plans and strategies are working. Nor can we use the input from our past efforts to refine the efforts that follow.

9. *Partnership.* Reaching an unreached people group is only the beginning ("a seed being planted," as Kaleb Jansen says). For that seed to grow into a strong indigenous church—especially in the unreached groups where Special Envoys will work—a partnership between that indigenous church and the outside Christian community must be built and maintained in every way possible. At the very least, such partnership must include ongoing focused prayer, intensified by a two-way flow of information.

Strategic Framework

Having presented the overall context of the nine steps of "a People becoming Christian,"[6] we can now spend the rest of the chapter elaborating on the strategy that Special Envoys will use as they identify (step two), adopt (step four) and then engage (step seven) the people group to which their prayer (step three) and their training (step six) have led them.

There is a lot of detail in this strategic framework. For clarity, I have tried to present it generally in the order in which Special Envoys might need to draw upon it as they first selected their group, then decided how best to approach it, and finally began their daily work, following their location and engagement within the group.

How to Enter

To assist Envoys as they begin to select and develop tactics for entering a given unreached people group, we can broadly generalize two kinds of populations in the world today and two corresponding approaches to them. To help differentiate these two populations, we'll measure four factors: hospitality of leadership, percentage of conversion, people's receptivity and need for development (see the examples on p. 89).

The *Hospitality Index* refers to the degree to which the leaders—of a country, of a cultural group within a country, or of a people group—are hospitable to Christianity. It refers especially to the quantity and severity of social (or governmental) sanctions placed upon gospel witness.

As noted earlier, a large proportion of the world's four billion non-Christians live in countries in which the leadership is resistive to the gospel. Many such countries have official policies prohibiting the entrance of evangelists and limiting or totally forbidding the evangelistic activities of national Christians. These sanctions on Christian witness and activity are placed on the minority Christian community by the leadership of the larger community.

The *Conversion Index* refers to the percentage of people within a given population who would identify themselves as Christians, especially in a safe environment where no persecution would be expected.

The *Receptivity Index* gauges how much the members of a particular population or people group are receptive to the gospel. Unlike the hospitality index, which refers to the relative absence of group or governmental sanctions on Christian witness and activity, the receptivity index reflects the relative openness to gospel witness among *individuals* within that group.

In the People's Republic of China, for instance, the hospitality index might be a mere one or two; according to recent reports, the government (the social setting) remains antagonistic toward Christian witness. However, the receptivity index might read six or seven; the people as a whole appear to be quite open to the gospel message.[7] Thus, hospitality is low, receptivity high. This level of disparity is not at all uncommon. In fact, it may be typical of many of the older and more authoritarian Communist regimes.

Finally, the *Development Index* seeks to measure the conditions of physical need in a target group and, more importantly, to measure whether there is a genuine need for physical relief and development assistance from outside sources.

Peter McPherson, formerly of the United States Agency for International Development, tells us that 90 percent of the world's population in the year 2000 will live in yet-to-be-developed countries. This means that potentially more people than ever will be living in an environment where their leadership will perceive a need for relief and development assistance from outside sources.[8]

It will often be difficult and somewhat subjective to establish openness scale ratings for a given country or people group, especially since in most unreached groups it would be impossible to survey the group members and their leadership. In such cases, missionaries or Special Envoys who have worked with these populations could be surveyed and asked to give their best guesses about the ratings for each of the four scales. Even though the final figures will not have a high level of demonstrable reliability, these "guestimated" ratings will still be quite helpful as a way of guiding us to the most appropriate mission strategies.

For diagnostic purposes, hospitality ratings averaging roughly seven and above should be considered highly open. Ratings averaging less than seven and more than five would be considered moderately open (or simply open). Groups or countries with hospitality ratings of five or less would be considered highly restricted—but, of course, still accessible through the plans Special Envoys employ.

The maximum imaginable level of hospitality, conversion, people's receptivity and need for development would be scored as a ten, moderate levels would be five, and so on. As specific countries and groups are evaluated, only a handful would be expected to rate at the lowest levels in all four categories. In most cases, even in relatively restricted-access countries, one would expect to see a divergence in these scales. That divergence would create the openings through which Special Envoys would enter the country or group to do their mission work.

Over the next few decades, it is hoped that the openness

model or some adaptation of it will prove to be a useful predictive and strategizing tool in the mission field. One might imagine a global mission computer somewhere containing regularly updated bar graphs depicting the four index levels for each of the world's sovereign and nonsovereign nations, as well as for each of its 5,310 unreached peoples. Through these models we could predict whether a country should receive Special Envoys (hospitality index five or less) or traditional missionaries (hospitality index above five), and whether it should be a provider of mission personnel for other lands (hospitality index of eight to ten).

In addition, the models would help us prescribe the best approaches for gaining access to the country or group, and, once there, for evangelizing with maximum effectiveness.

Finally, the models could be used to measure progress (step eight, assessment), through updating at regular intervals.

The Openness Model

Using four indices as guides (as shown in the accompanying charts), we can classify a given nation or people group relatively accurately as to the quality of its receptivity to evangelism.

The purpose of this classification is to identify openings within a two-hungers people group that will best enable Special Envoys to enter and then effectively evangelize within that group. A quick glance at the "Openness Index—China and Japan" reveals that the specific indices within it represent windows of opportunity—the openings through which Envoys can enter and move into effective evangelism.

Like the tiny "eye of the needle" doorway used as the nighttime entrance through biblical Jerusalem's walls, a single measure of three or more may provide sufficient opening for a Special Envoy to enter— though certainly not with a passport stamped "Missionary."

The People's Republic of China is an excellent example of the kind of restricted-access country where the government's hospitality index is very low, but the people's receptivity index is quite high. The rapid growth of Christianity in the P.R.C. is eloquent testimony to the opportunity that such a disparity can bring.

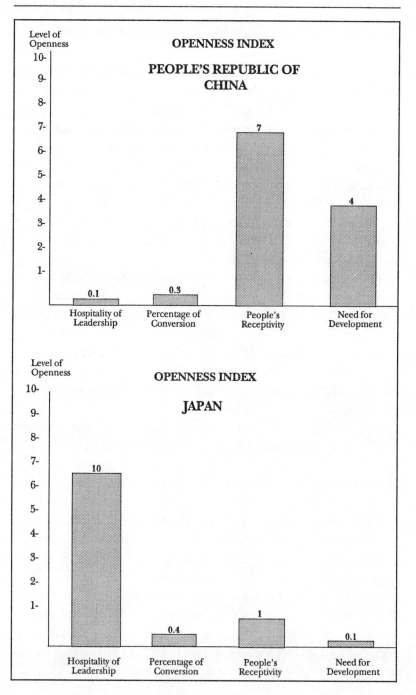

Analyzing Opportunities Within Subordinate Ethnic Groups
Given the fact that many unreached peoples are ethnic minorities within the nations where they live, a next potential strategic decision may involve the tactics to use in reaching a given subordinate ethnic group. There are basically two approaches, the *assimilationist* and the *identificational*. The assimilationist is the traditional method used by majority churches attempting to integrate ethnic minorities into their membership. The identificational approach promotes the development of distinct, monoethnic churches and missions. It is becoming increasingly popular and effective, especially as the level of identity moves downward from the nation-state to ethnicities more or less located within it.

The assimilationist approach is most effective with people of low intensity ethnic consciousness and is least effective with people of high intensity ethnic consciousness. The identificational approach, on the other hand, is most effective in working with people groups of moderate to high ethnic consciousness. (I define "ethnic consciousness" as the intensity of awareness of one's distinct peoplehood based on race, religion and/or national origin.)

To help identify the relative intensity of ethnic consciousness within a homogeneous people group—and thus to establish the approach that will be most successful in evangelizing within it—consider each of the items on the accompanying "Measure of Ethnic Consciousness" chart. Then select a number to represent that point on the continuum which best reflects the various characteristics of the particular ethnic group being approached.

If the *general* trend of the responses is toward the left side of the scale, there is a generally lower intensity of ethnic consciousness, and the assimilationist approach to reaching the group will tend to be more productive. If, however, the majority of characteristics tend toward the center or right end of the scale, research suggests that one or a combination of the identificational approaches to reaching this group will be more successful.

Special Envoys can use this "Measure of Ethnic Consciousness" to create a pointer that will guide them in selection of the most effective evangelization approach for their particular unreached people group.

MEASURE OF ETHNIC CONSCIOUSNESS

(Lower)		(Higher)
High cultural adaptability	1-2-3-4-5-6-7	Low cultural adaptability
The estalishment mentality ("I am here to stay")	1-2-3-4-5-6-7	The sojourner mentality ("I plan to go home")
Weak native religious identity	1-2-3-4-5-6-7	Strong native religious identity
High aspiration to assimilate	1-2-3-4-5-6-7	Low aspiration to assimilate
Loss of contact with the community of one's own kind	1-2-3-4-5-6-7	Contact with the community of one's own kind
Nonexistence of culturally bounded social organizations (clubs, community centers, associations)	1-2-3-4-5-6-7	Existence of culturally bounded social organizations
Nonexistence of culturally bounded mass media (ethnic language newspapers, radio, TV)	1-2-3-4-5-6-7	Existence of culturally bounded mass media
Lesser social distance (attitude)	1-2-3-4-5-6-7	Greater social distance (attitude)
Disappearance of racial discrimination (behavioral)	1-2-3-4-5-6-7	Persistence of racial discrimination (behavioral)
Lack of pride in national heritage	1-2-3-4-5-6-7	Pride in national heritage
Area with high degree of race mixing	1-2-3-4-5-6-7	Area with low degree of race mixing
Exogamous marriages common	1-2-3-4-5-6-7	Endogamous marriages common
The second, fourth or later generation	1-2-3-4-5-6-7	The immigrant generation or the third generation
Frequent change of last name	1-2-3-4-5-6-7	Pride in one's name
Upward social mobility	1-2-3-4-5-6-7	Minimal upward social mobility
Dispersion of the people in the region	1-2-3-4-5-6-7	Concentration of the people in the region
Absence of "power movements"	1-2-3-4-5-6-7	Presence of "power movements"
Low consciousness in one's national lineage	1-2-3-4-5-6-7	High consciousness in one's national lineage
Residence in a community of under 15% ethnic	1-2-3-4-5-6-7	Residence in a community over 50% ethnic

Two Other Basic Approaches

To clarify our understanding of the wide variety of strategies available to the Special Envoys, it may be helpful first to subdivide all possible strategies into two basic categories—*harvesting* approaches and *preparatory* approaches.

The harvesting approaches will be practiced primarily by traditional missionaries—in countries and people groups with higher hospitality ratings (above five). Here missionaries are allowed to enter as missionaries, there is a high receptivity to the gospel, Christians are well represented in the national population, and physical needs are not so great that they overwhelm all other concerns. In such cases, God's Word can and must be shared directly and aggressively.

As I have stated before, the world's exploding non-Christian population demands more, not fewer, traditional career missionaries to accelerate the harvesting in these groups and countries where harvesting strategies are feasible. These missionaries both deserve and need the increasingly sophisticated mission strategy training being provided in many quarters. They also need more precise knowledge of the processes by which peoples of the world come to faith and obedience in Jesus Christ. Because of the rapid urbanization and Asianization of the world's population, many of these future career missionaries also will require specialized training in techniques for reaching specific people groups in the cities and in the more open parts of Asia.

The preparatory approaches—doing something now in the hope that people will respond to the gospel later—usually will be the approaches of choice for God's Special Envoys. These are usually the Envoys' best alternatives among populations with hospitality ratings averaging five or less.

Where career missionaries are not permitted to enter, where people are least responsive to the gospel, where few or no known Christians are part of the population, where people are in need of food, basic health care, education and information on proper nutrition and food production—in these places God's Special

Envoys can be very effective in a quiet way, by letting their light so shine before men and women that they may see their good works and glorify their Father who is in heaven (Mt 5:16).

Special Envoys, much more than traditional missionaries, will often maintain a distinction between public strategy and the one employed in private, on a one-on-one basis with individual prospective converts. Here the Envoy may harvest—but very discreetly—being careful to nurture and protect the inquirer until he or she is strong enough in the faith to withstand the repression that frequently follows conversion.

Often, building a one-on-one friendship works positively toward leading a person to Christ. The multiplication of this process may eventually create not one Christ group but many. Then, as these Christ groups are formed, some of the same principles may apply that have been found to lead to the growth and replication of individual churches in other areas.

Principles for Christ Group Growth

For more than three decades I have been exploring the question of how God brings people of varied cultural backgrounds to faith and obedience in Christ. Naturally, no two cases of church growth are exactly alike. The growth pattern of a church in Punjab, India, differs from that of a church in Tokyo or in Garden Grove, California. Yet repeated investigations show that several of the same factors are found in most of the case studies of rapidly growing churches. These factors appear to have stimulated the growth of a significant number of churches that have been the subject of my past studies—in Japan, Brazil, Ethiopia, Indonesia and the United States.

I believe that Special Envoys will be able to make good use of these same principles in the countries and people groups where they will work. Where an established church is already operating within these areas, the same principles could be expected to have a positive influence on the growth of these churches, just as they have in other parts of the world.

In most cases, however, the Special Envoys' goal will be to promote the growth of Christ groups. With this in mind, I have modified these principles slightly to attune them better to the situations Special Envoys will face. The following factors would be expected to stimulate the growth of Christ groups:

1. *Growth-oriented philosophy of ministry.* A Christ group likely to grow will possess a clearly delineated philosophy of ministry bent on growth. This philosophy drives every member of the group to witness to the unsaved and affirms the expansion of God's kingdom through multiplying these Christ groups and, whenever possible, converting a Christ group into an indigenous church.

2. *Dynamic witnessing members.* A Christ group likely to grow is made up of numerous dynamic witnessing members in frequent contact with non-Christians in their community. The leader of the Christ group exerts his or her influence to make sure a proportionately large number of "outreach laypeople" are recruited, trained and sent out into the community. (A nongrowing Christ group or church, in contrast, mobilizes its lay leaders primarily for the maintenance of that group or church as an institution—serving on committees and making sure the group operates smoothly.)

3. *An accurate understanding of itself and its community.* A Christ group likely to grow has an accurate knowledge of its own membership constituency and the community surrounding it. Sophisticated questionnaires and polling techniques are not required here. In most cases, it will be enough for the leadership of the Christ group to know what kind of people have joined the group for the past few years and, thus, among whom it is most effective.

4. *Respecting the lines of communication.* Christ groups, like churches, grow by respecting lines of communication—knowing that the gospel often flows best from one member of a family to another or between two friends. Research among churches shows that the overwhelming majority of most congregations

(and we would assume Christ groups as well) have become Christians or joined a particular worshiping body because of the prior involvement of their Christian relatives or friends.

5. *The constant search for God's bridges.* A Christ group likely to grow is in constant search for "God's bridges," and, upon their discovery, develops strategies to each of them. The patriarch of church growth thinking, Dr. Donald McGavran, uses the phrase "bridges of God" to refer to the segments of society that at a given time are most responsive to the gospel. The nature of these bridges may vary, depending on the culture and the situation, but they always exist. Some examples might be people who have just been divorced, who are experiencing a financial crisis, who have lost a child due to suicide, who are being persecuted, who have become refugees, or who for any reason are strongly dissatisfied with their situation or themselves.

6. *Systems of incorporating and training new members.* A Christ group likely to grow will develop effective systems of incorporating and training new members. Such groups grow when they take in new members on a steady basis, rapidly incorporating them into the core life of the group, nurturing them to become productive and responsive members, and motivating them onward to increasing levels of commitment and involvement.

7. *A high premium on prayer.* A Christ group likely to grow will place a high premium on prayer and consequently on the Holy Spirit. It is prayer-led and Spirit-filled. In my studies of church growth in five different countries, I have yet to see a rapidly growing church that has not emphasized intense prayer on the part of its members, both individually and corporately. Especially in the restrictive and hazardous contexts in which Special Envoys will operate, a high premium on prayer and the Holy Spirit will be absolutely essential for Christ group growth.

My research has indicated that these seven basic principles would be likely to influence growth in Christ groups and, most certainly, in an indigenous church, if such were available. To these I would like to add three more principles suggested by

C. Peter Wagner in his article, "Three Growth Principles for a Soul-winning Church."[9] While there is some obvious overlap between my own principles and those suggested by Wagner, I think he offers particularly good insights, the benefits of which are well worth the possible duplication.

These three points do not claim to be a fair summarization of Wagner's thinking, but rather are abstractions from it, collected to shed additional light on principles that should help stimulate the growth of Christ groups.

1. A dedicated leader committed to leading the church group into growth. There is a high price required of the leader of any worshiping body if that body is to grow, Wagner says. The first price: hard work. The second: the willingness to share leadership. This sharing should not take place at the level of top leadership, Wagner explains, but rather at all levels below. As Wagner states, "Gifted lay leadership needs to be discovered and trained and put to work."[10]

The third price that leaders of growing Christ groups must pay is "a willingness to have church members whom they cannot personally pastor." This will become increasingly necessary as a Christ group grows or, more likely, subdivides into additional Christ groups. When that happens, the leader must be willing to move from what has been called a "shepherd" attitude to a "rancher" attitude. A rancher sees to it that all the people are properly cared for and counseled and consoled, but does not attempt to do it personally. He recruits and trains others who are gifted for that task so that his own energies can be used for more crucial and specialized leadership roles.[11]

2. A worshiping body willing to pay the price for growth. The price for growth that the members of the Christ group must be willing to pay takes three forms: "willingness to follow growth leadership" of the Christ group leader; willingness to make generous contributions of their own funds and time so that growth takes place; and willingness "to readjust their fellowship patterns in order to make newcomers feel welcome."[12]

3. Willingness to seek help. This final principle is Wagner's suggestion that the leadership of worshiping bodies should be willing to seek outside assistance promptly if that body is not growing. Naturally, Special Envoys will probably find such assistance far less readily available than would a pastor in his native land. Yet Envoys who are willing to ask for help may well be able to find a more experienced evangelist who is already located in the Envoy's area of operation and can offer valuable suggestions.

I would make two suggestions to the Envoy facing such circumstances. First, the Envoy must be willing to admit that a problem exists and be humble enough to seek guidance. Second, the Envoy needs to be willing to seek assistance, even if the adviser's ecclesiastical orientation happens to be slightly different from his or her own.

A Few Other Reminders
This is probably a good time to make plain that Special Envoy tactics should certainly include prompt sharing of all findings about the techniques that appear to be effective in this new and as yet inadequately researched field. In this practice we are following the lead of church growth strategists, one of whose tenets has been that potentially useful church growth research should be shared rapidly—sometimes even at a less-than-fully refined stage—to accelerate the generation of new knowledge. (Both chapter twelve and the bibliography describe publications that can provide Special Envoys with current mission research and give them an avenue for publishing some of their own findings. Naturally, the bulletin chosen should be instructed to protect the anonymity of Special Envoys and their disciples who are attempting to spread the gospel in sensitive areas.)

In inhospitable circumstances, the Christ groups (including house churches and other quasi-church forms) arising out of the Envoys' work might have to assume more of an underground approach than would otherwise be required. Traditionally, the approach has been that if a person is not sincere enough to risk persecution for Christ's sake, he or she is not really ready to become a Christian. Under some circumstances, I believe this is still the correct position; but in others it may not be. The point is that the mission field of the Special Envoys will require flexibility and some compromises as well.

For example, a Christian willing to serve—and who already is working in a restricted-access country—probably should be commissioned immediately as a pro tem Special Envoy and then encouraged to pursue independent instruction to secure the additional training required. An agricultural specialist who has already been employed by the government of a limited-access country might serve effectively until additional training could be acquired. He could hold regular Bible studies in his home. Possibly, he could also selectively distribute Scripture and tracts, written in the native ("heart") tongue.

In many situations, Special Envoys will need to have the adaptability to work in tandem with Third World missionaries. In 1990, David Barrett calculated that there were thirty-eight thousand foreign missionaries sent out by "developing countries outside the Western and Communist worlds."[13]

The following reports by Jeleta Fryman suggest the extent of the expanding work of these Third World missionaries.

Even after the government of Mozambique turned Communist, one Malawi missionary continued to cross the border regularly, preaching about the Lord. He planted thirty-five churches before the government soldiers arrested him and refused to let him enter Mozambique any more.

Chinese churches in Singapore sent Bible translators to northern Thailand.

The Church of Uganda expanded its foreign missionary efforts considerably during the persecutions of Idi Amin's tyrannical regime.

In spite of intense persecution within its own country, the Church in El Salvador supports missionaries to Spain. And in one economically difficult year, El Salvador's Iglesia Nazaret

(Nazareth Church) increased its foreign mission budget 41 percent.

In northeast India, Christians reportedly cross the borders regularly to travel and preach in Burma and as far east as China. While the number of missionaries to India has decreased 40 percent in the past fifteen years, India's own cross-cultural ministry force has swelled to 2,277.

Significant world mission efforts also are being fielded by the Church in Burma, in Malaysia, in Brazil, and especially in South Korea.[14]

Thus, Special Envoys who can learn to work successfully with their brother and sister missionaries from the "uttermost parts" of the world will find their own effectiveness greatly increased.

Missiologist Peter Wagner predicted, quite conservatively I think, that there could be more than 50,000 of these missionaries originating from the Third World by the year 2000.[15] For only a few years later, another study predicted over 150,000.[16] We can hope that a significant portion of them will join the effort to reach unreached non-Christians in unreached people groups—especially in situations where Third World missionaries have cultural commonalities with members of the target groups.

Some new skills will also have to be developed in order to train disciples who can independently create new churches or Christ groups, without additional assistance from the Envoy or an outside group. This is the somewhat elusive ability to produce "spontaneous expansion." Roland Allen described this process in *The Spontaneous Expansion of the Church,* a book published in 1927 but still relevant today. As Allen described it,

> The rapid and wide expansion of the Church in the early centuries was due . . . mainly to the spontaneous activity of individuals. . . . As men moved about there were constantly springing up new groups of Christians in different places.
>
> The Church expanded simply by organizing these little groups as they were converted, handing on to them the organization which she had received from her first founders.

... By a simple act the new group was brought into the unity of the Church, and equipped, as its predecessors had been equipped, not only with all the spiritual power and authority necessary for its own life as an organized unit, but also with all the authority needed to repeat the same process whenever one of its members might convert men in any new village or town.[17]

The actual process of spontaneous expansion is often quite subtle and certainly somewhat mysterious; however, as even this brief quote makes clear, there are always three basic preconditions to the process: First, the powerful involvement of the Holy Spirit. Second, the prompt release of authority and control by the conversion agent (the missionary or Envoy). Third, the willingness to just "let things happen," without trying to control the process or the doctrine, or without trying to take credit for or provide centralized management for the groups once they have sprung up.

Clearly, spontaneous expansion works. It was the primary method of all church growth until about A.D. 950. Also, equally clearly, it requires gospel propagators who will be willing to start the process and then let go, even to the extent of waiving requirements for ordination, establishing "proper" doctrine, and the like.

Some Final Tips

Finally, here are a number of other approaches that I think will prove effective for the Special Envoys:

1. *Relationship evangelism.* Much of the Special Envoys' evangelism will have to be expressed in the contexts of individual relationships rather than groups. This style has sometimes been called "friendship" evangelism. It will require great patience on the Envoy's part, building trust slowly and showing Christian virtues more often through deeds than words. This is what has been called the more "personal" evangelism style of Jesus rather than the "proclamational" style of John the Baptist.[18]

2. Thinking small. In countries where the founding of churches is initially both a dangerous and an unrealistic goal, Special Envoys will have to think in terms of far more humble worship forms, such as regular meetings in homes or in other relatively safe environments.

For validation of the effectiveness of this strategy, the Envoys might do well to remember Dr. Paul Yonggi Cho, pastor of what may be the world's largest church, Yoido Island Full Gospel Church in Seoul, Korea. In 1989 it had 504,250 members—most of whom participate through some forty-four thousand Christ groups (called "cells" within that church), led by the church's lay ministers in private homes.[19]

Development worker John Huffaker, working in the Segalo refugee camp in Somalia, has reported that his most successful evangelization occurred while sitting under a riverside tree near the camp. In that picturesque setting, Huffaker held a regular Bible study with five or six refugee men. At first the Bible studies took place inside one of the grass houses in the refugee camp. When things became tense within the camp, and the men were afraid of other people finding out about their study of the Word, they suggested the new location beneath the tree.

By being sensitive to locations preferred by the people being ministered to, the Special Envoy not only can become more effective but perhaps also can have a more enriching spiritual experience of his or her own.

3. Accepting local nationalism and cultural values. Except where it clearly conflicts with direct teachings of the Bible, Envoys will have to discard some of their own culturally biased ideas of "proper Christianity" and allow new converts to develop a Christian belief and worship style compatible with their culture, which permits pride in their own nation and its traditions. The goal is to bring the maximum number of people to faith and obedience in Christ. To this end, the Envoy must give up some personal, culturally biased values so that the resulting Christ groups are truly indigenous, and thus truly relevant to surrounding culture.

4. Being supportive of the local administration. As difficult as it may be sometimes, Special Envoys must avoid attacking the local government. Their goal is to promote the kingdom and redemption through Christ, not to attack political systems or other religions.

In the long term, only Envoys whom the government feels are relatively harmless to them will be permitted to succeed. These Envoys will need to have a positive message and a positive ministry. Their model should be Jesus telling us to "give to Caesar what is Caesar's, and to God what is God's" (Lk 20:25). Another model could be the apostle Paul, through whom God worked in Ephesus to convert many thousands without Paul's ever once attacking the goddess held sacred by that city's leaders (Acts 19:37).

The diplomatic implication of the last word of the title "God's Special Envoys" is quite deliberate. Political savvy is required. In most cases, the Envoys will need to be aware of political realities at the national level of the countries where they work, as well as being astute about politics within the local villages or communities where their ministries actually take place.

5. Being relevant. To be understood and believed, the Envoys need to understand the values of the culture where they work. More important, they must be able to explain the gospel with analogies that fit the value structure and needs of the people they wish to convert. As members of the minority wherever they work, Envoys must know a great deal about the dominant religious or political philosophy they are attempting to supplant.

It would appear, for example, that an animist's selection of either Islam or Christianity will depend on the degree to which the "new religion" is made culturally relevant to him. This relevance would not usually be expressed in any philosophical statements from the Special Envoys, but more likely by their actions, especially in areas such as relief and development. For an animist, a development approach that preserved and respected nature and God's natural gifts might be vital. Conversely, a religious approach that attempts to separate a human being's spiritual development from the physical world might have no relevance at all.[20]

Likewise, Envoys must learn to speak the language of need. If they cannot tailor their ministries to the often overwhelming physical and emotional needs of the people they hope to reach, these people will probably not be reached at all.

This point is underlined by the success of an outreach of the First Christian Reformed Church operating within an urban slum in Tegucigalpa, the capital of Honduras. Early on, the church realized that to evangelize effectively, "discipleship classes had to be related to the needs of the people." Among the target population, 30 percent were unemployed and 45 percent were illiterate. In reponse to these needs the church established the John Calvin Technical Institute. The instructors are all professing Christians with very practical skills. In 1982 when the school opened, 37 students were enrolled. By early 1983 there were 144 students, taking courses in electronics, electricity, tailoring, carpentry and fashion design. The school's ministry is symbiotic. The classes are practical and geared directly to the target group's need for jobs.

On the spiritual side, however, each class day begins with a ten-minute Bible study. There is a youth program on Saturdays, and a program for adults has been organized. As of this report, sixteen persons were attending the church's prebaptismal classes, and more were expected to make a commitment to Christ soon.[21]

6. Being ready. Our Lord must often have been weary in his ministry, yet he was always ready to speak of his Father and the kingdom, whenever the right situation presented itself. The Special Envoy must also be prepared to take advantage of every opportunity the Lord provides to share the gospel. In *The Ethics of Smuggling*, Brother Andrew cites many personal experiences to illustrate this point.

My favorite of his examples occurred when his Volkswagen

bus was seized in the formerly Russian-occupied zone between Berlin and West Germany. While searching the bus's contents, one of the guards discovered Brother Andrew's flannel-graph Bible characters and inquired what their purpose was. Andrew proceeded to do a flannel-graph presentation from Ephesians 6 before a room full of Red Army guards. He had time to give a powerful witness before the officer in charge realized Brother Andrew was preaching and angrily told him to get back in his bus and leave.[22]

In many restrictive countries, Special Envoys will need to have the courage and presence of mind to capitalize on opportunities such as these. God will provide the opportunities, if the Envoy is looking for them and is open to the Holy Spirit's instruction on how to proceed.

Obviously, the mission strategy of the Special Envoys requires new approaches, plus great patience, great love and the sowing of many seeds—with the prayer that God will do the watering.

With this thought in mind, let us next look at some refinements in the Special Envoy strategy for people groups where physical needs are great.

Questions for Thought and Review
1. Explain the Openness Model and how it works.
2. Name some basic techniques for building Christ groups.
3. List some of the elements in the Special Envoy strategy that seem most important to you.

7
How the Strategy Is Refined to Meet Physical Needs

In *BEYOND HUNGER,* ART BEALS, FORMER EXECUTIVE DIRECTOR for World Concern, reports seeing a powerful Christian ministry among refugees in the heavily Muslim nation of Somalia. Traditional Christian missionary activities there were considered impossible; helpers in the refugee camp were Christians, but certainly not missionaries. They were medical professionals, a cook, an engineer, a midwife, a pharmacist.

Yet with extensive training in their skill areas, and with "the love of Jesus burning in their souls—they came to bring hope and health, nurture and nutrition to these refugees who had suffered so much." Even without a church planter or evangelist among the whole group of Christian workers, "the witness was unmistakable, quiet and strong, compassionate and sure. Thousands of Somalians were exposed to the reality of God's love."[1]

A more detailed picture of a similarly effective ministry in

Somalia is given by development worker John Huffaker. After 1.5 million refugees fled from famine and war in neighboring Ethiopia in the late 1970s, thirty-three volunteer agencies were invited to Somalia to conduct relief and development work among them. Six of these agencies were Christian, including Food for the Hungry.

In a report for the Symbiotic Ministries Symposium at Biola University in March 1985,[2] Huffaker said that Food for the Hungry's initial strategy involved setting up supplementary feeding programs in two refugee camps with a combined population of ninety thousand. This effort was directed toward malnourished children and pregnant and nursing mothers. As the relief situation improved, the staff sensed a need for new development projects aimed at building self-sufficiency. Three such projects were developed.

The first provided seeds, tools and irrigation supplies to groups of twenty families. The second helped a group of women design ceramic stoves that could cut their fuel consumption up to 50 percent (a vital economy, because of deforestation in the area). Widows without other means of support were taught how to fabricate the stoves and then market them in their communities. The third project helped establish small businesses—aiding a former baker with a loan so he could build an oven, providing tools to beekeepers to carry on their trade, and assisting refugee widows in poultry production. These small business efforts evolved out of relief projects already in progress.

Much of the design for these programs grew out of consultations with camp and community leaders. The agricultural project, for example, developed from refugee requests for assistance in obtaining seeds and tools. In the ceramic stove project, appropriate local technology was refined to address the local shortage of fuel. The result was that some women needed to walk only five hours, rather than the usual ten, to secure a typically adequate supply of wood.

In addition, some of the women in the ceramic stove project

eventually asked to be taught about the Bible. Somalia prohibited proselytizing and direct evangelization of Muslims, and it was Food for the Hungry's intent to comply with this law. However, as Huffaker states, "Within the context of our work, if individuals approached us with questions about our faith, we felt completely at liberty to share with them the gospel of Jesus Christ." While operating fully within the letter of Somali law, the Food for the Hungry program in that country nevertheless found ample opportunities for evangelism and discipling.

For example, in Mogadishu, the capital of Somalia, where Food for the Hungry was headquartered, the staff participated in an international fellowship called "Christ Church" and also in the National Believers' Fellowship. A Bible study was instituted for several refugees who had secured work and residence in the capital.

At the outset, the government knew that Food for the Hungry was a Christian relief and development organization. It was never Food for the Hungry's intention to hide Christian activities from either the government leaders or the refugees themselves. Instead, Huffaker says, "We conducted Bible studies in our homes and in the homes of other national believers and asked or answered questions when it was appropriate. At no time were we threatened by any of the national population because of our beliefs."

In one of the refugee camps where Food for the Hungry worked, a group of approximately forty believers was found. They had been meeting twice a week for prayer and worship—having only one small pocket New Testament for their use. Food for the Hungry began teaching basic biblical concepts to the group members and provided them with additional Bibles. The group appeared to experience a revival, and some who had left it earlier and converted to Islam were found returning to worship with the Christians.

Through contacts made in the agricultural work and ceramic stove projects, several refugees made new or renewed commitments to Christ. One of these had heard the gospel as a child from a mission school in his homeland. Yet at the time he did not feel he had a sufficient understanding to make a commitment to Christ, and he had prayed for someone to come and present to him clearly the Christian faith. Now in a refugee camp twenty-five years later, "he came to our house to have tea," Huffaker recalls, "and asked us to explain to him what it meant to be a Christian."

Christians in a nearby town asked Food for the Hungry to conduct a weekly Bible study for them. Two believers from the camp traveled to the town with Food for the Hungry staff, resulting in a small group of five or six who would sit out under a tree or in a grass hut to have tea, study Scripture, and join together in prayer.

Huffaker's study of the process of refugee conversions in Somalia suggests a number of thoughts about strategies that appear to work best in these refugee situations. The following is taken from Huffaker's report, with italics added by me.

In working with the refugees we attempted to *live at the same level of lifestyle* that the refugees lived. There were, of course, limitations to the extent to which this could be done. Our intention was to make our home as comfortable for the refugees as possible, in other words, avoid setting up barriers. The refugees and villagers were welcome to visit us and did not feel threatened by our lifestyle. In turn, they did not feel uncomfortable in inviting us to their homes. Our grass huts and dirt floors also proved to be more practical for staying cool in the heat of the desert.

By working initially in a relief setting when the going was tough and by living alongside the refugees, we *established credibility*. People saw the nitty-gritty of our daily lives and recognized that we did not have ulterior motives for doing our work. As we *worked with local leadership and developed relationships*, the refugees began to acknowledge us as human beings very much like themselves. Our own growth in understanding their language and culture was a continual process.

Our lifestyle within both camps as well as in the capital city created a stark contrast to other relief/development workers. For example, in Camp #2 there was a medical team that averaged four to ten workers. Their lifestyle, their words, and their work were very much in contrast with *the integrity and personal concern we communicated.* The contrast drew some interesting remarks from refugees who wanted to know why all Americans were not alike. It certainly presented opportunities to talk about value differences.

In 1983, Muslim medical teams set up work in many refugee camps. Their clinics were manned by devout Bengali doctors. The refugees began commenting on the difference between these noncaring doctors and our listening and responsive team. Again, this contrast *provided opportunities to discuss religious differences.*

Our ministry seemed to "take root" among refugees or villagers who had previously been exposed to the gospel or the concept of Christianity. Several refugees in Camp #2 remembered the medical work of other missionaries in their homeland. Others had attended some form of church in their past. This background gave them at least a framework with which to develop new ideas and understandings of the Scriptures. On several occasions, we were *reaping the seed that had been sown by others* in earlier years.[3]

In Somalia, Huffaker says, "we were performing what I call 'tea shop evangelism,'" which amounts to observing when and where social exchanges take place and recognizing the ideal time for giving and taking of thoughts, questions and ideas.

It was a matter of acknowledging the human value of those whom we are working with and among, and becoming their friends. The more we learned from them, the more they were willing to learn from us. There are very few people in the world who do not respond to genuine warmth, interest, curiosity, and desire for friendship.

Reasons for Success

It's not yet completely clear why evangelism integrated with relief and development work is so effective—but it is, as shown by the above illustrations from Somalia. We can, however, point to several plausible causes for the increased harvest for the Lord that occurs when, under proper circumstances, evangelism is paired with relief and development.

To begin with, there are some very basic reasons a missionary evangelist should feel compelled to be involved in relief and development. I have reproduced a few of these in the accompanying scriptural sampling, pairing them with our equally pressing instructions to evangelize. (I hope you will take time to look up and ponder these passages, reflecting especially on their frequent coexistence, especially in the ministry of our Lord.)

From the passages in the scriptural sampling, you'll see that helping those in physical need is one of the most fundamental duties of all Christians and one of the responsibilities most consistently stressed throughout Scripture.

Ted Engstrom, former president of World Vision, described the process of relief and development as "an integral part of our obedience to 'go into all the world.'"[4] I agree with him completely.

You'll also find that relief and development provide some of the most fruitful opportunities for conversions, especially in people groups that would be hard for traditional missionaries to penetrate. Equally important, Christian relief and development can help us reach large numbers of human beings who otherwise would probably live and die without Christ.

In *Beyond Hunger* Art Beals says,

Working with the "new missionary," the relief and development professional, I have seen doors once closed to the gospel swing wide open. . . . As God's love becomes incarnated once again in the flesh and blood of his compassionate children, giving the "cup of cold water in my name" becomes a powerful instrument for Christian witness.[5]

A Scriptural Sampling of Why We Respond to *Both* Physical and Spiritual Needs

Some Instructions to Respond to Physical Needs
Leviticus 25:35
Deuteronomy 15:7-11
Psalm 41:1
Proverbs 11:25; 14:21, 31; 19:17; 22:9; 28:27; 29:7; 31:8-9
Isaiah 10:1-2; 58:6-7
Micah 6:8
Matthew 5:16; 7:12; 10:8; 25:40
Mark 12:44
Luke 3:11; 6:38; 9:48; 10:30-37; 11:41; 12:33-34
Acts 20:35
Romans 12:8, 13, 20
2 Corinthians 9:7
Galatians 5:6; 6:2, 9-10
1 Timothy 6:18-19
Hebrews 13:16
James 2:15-17
1 John 3:17

Some Instructions to Respond to Spiritual Needs
Matthew 4:19; 24:14; 28:19
Mark 16:15
Luke 24:46-47
John 4:35; 20:21; 21:15-17
Acts 1:8
Romans 16:26
Revelation 5:9-10

This is especially true in situations involving refugees fleeing large-scale disasters. Wars, famines, floods and the condition of being uprooted all create a level of dissatisfaction with the status quo that seems to open people's hearts and minds to a rare degree. As they become displaced, their ties to their background seem to loosen; they become willing to consider philosophical alternatives (such as Christianity) that under other circumstances might be perceived as too alien to even think about.

In addition, relief and development allow us to show forth the body of Christ at its loving and cooperating best. Many disaster relief situations bring together a community of exemplary Christians who, in many cases, are both trained evangelists and representatives of the body at its finest. The people they are helping experience a superior level of Christian behavior, highly consistent with scriptural teaching, creating a persuasive presence for Christ.

Moreover, this presence is heightened by the perception that the government appears to be supporting Christianity, even in countries that normally are antagonistic. This greater public tolerance of Christianity may often be more than temporary. Relief and development allow us to demonstrate loving, nonpolitical and genuinely benevolent intentions in ways that may persuade local and national governments to be more receptive to Christian missionaries later on. But at least for the time being, the refugees sense their freedom to learn from Christians without government retribution.

Under these circumstances, evangelistic results can be astounding. In 1980 I visited Thailand's Khao-I-Dang refugee camp for Cambodian war refugees just inside the Thai border. There were 130,000 suffering refugees in the camp, of whom only eight families had been Christian at the beginning. But soon conversions began occurring sometimes at the rate of hundreds a day. I witnessed the dynamic worship of the believers there and had the privilege of preaching both in their church and among smaller groups. Within months, the Christian population of Khao-I-Dang had grown to twenty thousand. Why this success?

One reason is the "bridge" created by the refugees' spiritual crisis at losing family, possessions and way of life. Clearly these people were open to a better answer and a better way. Cynics might ascribe the conversions to the refugees' desire to gain credentials that would make them more attractive candidates for immigration to the United States. Opportunist conversion may have been a factor, of course, but it by no means could account for the massive numbers who came to Christ at Khao-I-Dang and at scores of other refugee camps I have visited.

As I review the studies of conversions in refugee camps throughout the world, a number of factors consistently emerge in those cases when conversion rates have been high:

1. *Quality and dedication of Christian staff.* For staff workers, the refugee camp routine is one of much hard work and many long hours. To succeed in having a spiritual impact on these refugees who have lost everything, they must exhibit a high level of dedication in both their Christian witness and their Christian service.

2. *Ability to get along well with authorities.* Many refugee camps are intensely political, and therefore highly regulated by national or local government officials of the host country. In such situations Christian relief and development workers must develop good skills in working with the officials. Often this involves compromise. It certainly requires a high level of diplomatic professionalism and the ability to coexist with authorities, respecting their right to maintain control in what is a difficult situation for all.

3. *Evangelistic skill.* Since refugees tend to be very open to Christ, the Christian worker in these circumstances must be competent enough in evangelism skills to give a clear picture of Christianity in a manner appropriate to deep-felt refugee needs. An academic approach is unsuitable; refugees are looking for answers, not new intellectual challenge.

4. *Relevance to cultural values.* Finally, Christian relief and development workers must be able to present Christianity in a manner fitting the refugees' native culture. The refugees must be able to sense that this is *their* religion, with a Lord who truly understands their unique needs.

Another advantage of relief and development is the benefit it brings to indigenous churches. If a church already has been established in the area in which we are helping, we can design distribution systems that utilize the church, increasing its ministry and prestige. In this situation the Christian relief and development agency would function as an enabler for the local church. We can help existing Christian churches and missions fulfill their ministry of reaching non-Christians by making available to them needed food commodities, necessary funds, and specialist personnel.

The relief and development agency also can function as an intermediary and a catalyst. Here we can use our information ministries to "plead the cause of the poor and needy" (Prov 31:9 KJV), mobilizing First World Christians to come to their support. The result is a more vigorous and effective global body of believers, with greater involvement by individual Christians in a symbiotic ministry that will ultimately bring more of the lost to Christ.

As we look into the future, we discover almost limitless opportunities for Special Envoys to work in contexts of human need. *Global 2000,* one of the most comprehensive studies to date of the expected status of the world in the year 2000, predicts that as the next century begins the world will be more crowded, more polluted, less stable ecologically and more vulnerable to more kinds of disturbances than is our world today.[6]

More than a half billion human beings are now chronically and consistently hungry, with nearly thirteen million expected to die from hunger and hunger-related causes this year. Every minute hunger claims another twenty-four lives, eighteen of them children. Thirty-five thousand die from hunger and related causes every day, 365 days a year.[7] Though some maintain that the world hunger situation is improving, there is little agreement on this point. In fact, some sources predict that the number of hungry people will double by the year 2000.[8]

I would maintain that the issue of how we respond to the massive needs of our fellow human beings is really far more important than arguing about whether or not it is humanly possible for these needs eventually to be extinguished. The fact is that thirty-five thousand people—most of them children—now die of hunger and related causes every day. It is also a fact that natural disasters, war and deadly disease continue at an alarming rate.

As Christians, we must continue to respond to these needs as best we can until the Lord returns. The real question—and our focus here—is: How can we respond to these needs while more effectively pursuing the Great Commission?

Tactics

From my own experience and the experience of others, I will now suggest a number of tactics that can help Special Envoys to meet physical needs effectively, while increasing the harvest for Christ. I have not listed these ideas in any particular order; rather, their actual order of importance will vary depending on the situation.

Note that the primary focus of these ideas is on development rather than relief. This is because during the relief phase of the relief-recovery-development-sustainability continuum (to be explained in chapter eight), there are rarely adequate opportunities for evangelization. This does not mean, however, that the relief phase is unimportant. Quite the contrary. If properly handled, it can create a climate of trust and mutual respect that will make later evangelistic efforts far more fruitful.

The following, then, are thirteen suggested tactics related to situations of need:

1. High selectivity in staffing. In relief and development situations there is always a limited budget, and—in restricted-access countries especially—often a limitation in the number of "expatriate" staff the host nation will allow you to bring in.

This means that every expatriate staff member must be the best-trained possible, since lives are at stake, both temporal and eternal. Great care should also be taken in selection of the national staff, since they are your best prospects for disciples who can continue the evangelism after the development team leaves.

In one restricted-access country where Food for the Hungry operates, three of our five relief and development teams have been headed by former missionaries—all with fluency in at least one of the local languages, all with graduate-level training, and all with at least ten years' prior mission experience in that same country. The director of our programs there has a master's degree in a relief-related field, has a long-term mission background, and is fluent in the local language.

If this sounds like overqualification, it isn't. These highly experienced professionals (all of whom meet Special Envoy standards) cost no more to maintain in the field than novices would. Yet with their more mature skills they have gained the respect of the local officials (normally anti-Christian) and have also maximized the results we can achieve.

2. *Impartial giving.* Hunger knows no religious or political distinctions, nor should development and relief. Aid should be given impartially to all who need it. When it is, both the recipients and their government will appreciate your even-handedness and will believe more in the disinterestedness of your concern.

In 1982, a combined effort of relief organizations and American and Canadian churches provided a massive relief effort in Poland, supplying food, medicine, clothing and Bibles. At Warsaw's Polaska Church—one of the main distribution points—aid was provided totally indiscriminately. There was no requirement that the recipients be Christian or even interested in learning more about Christ. By coincidence, the church was next door to a large police station, so we had ample opportunity to satisfy the government as to the benign and helpful nature of this aid.

The Reverend George Bajenski reported that membership of the Polaska Church doubled within three years. Bajenski also said that there appeared to be a general growth in Christian witness in other parts of Poland, and the Polish government seemed increasingly receptive to the presence of evangelical Christian groups.[9]

We have learned from Poland—through repeated trips back to that country and from Pastor Bajenski's later interviews—that people long remember good deeds, especially unselfish ones. A genuine act of charity offered impartially to all who need assistance is truly an investment in the future with long-term dividends.

3. Staying nonpolitical. It sometimes takes great discipline, but if you want to operate effectively in a restricted country, you've got to avoid taking sides. The top priority for Special Envoys should be to win converts for the eternal kingdom, not to reform a temporal one. By taking sides against the government, the Envoys risk scaring away potential converts who, after all, might prefer to learn about Christ without landing in jail.

A question sometimes raised is why we help in countries that potentially are our enemies. The first answer comes from the Bible: "If your enemy is hungry, give him food to eat; if he is thirsty, give him water to drink" (Prov 25:21). Another answer is that we help people, not their governments. Likewise, it is those same people (not their governments) whom we wish to evangelize.

Finally, there's the perspective of our own national interest. Arthur Simon, founder and director of Bread for the World, makes this point:

> Aside from our moral perspective as Christians, it is not in our national interest to use food as a political weapon. We do not endear ourselves to other nations in this way. If we withhold food from starving people in Ethiopia because we don't like their government, do we make Ethiopians more likely to tilt toward the West and an open society? Or do we make them all the more determined to head in the opposite direction? No one can say for certain, and we should do right regardless of the consequences. But certainly there is a greater possibility that the country will eventually lean in our direction if we are perceived as people who have compassion for their starving citizens.[10]

What Simon says should apply not only to the national interest of the United States but to other democratic countries in the world.

4. Not rushing the evangelism. Before people from another culture will believe the things we say, they need concrete demonstrations of our genuine care for them. This is the first reason that evangelism usually should not begin the moment Special Envoys arrive on the scene of a disaster. The second reason derives from human physiology. As one medical missionary from Ethiopia put it, hungry people cannot hear a spiritual message "until you get some food in their stomachs."[11]

The missionary's statement, by the way, is literally correct. By the time a hunger situation has grown severe enough for the international community to be involved, the realistic possibilities for immediate evangelism tend to be limited. With severe and prolonged hunger, the body literally eats its own muscle and tissue, until all that remains is a skin-draped skeleton with staring eyes and very little capacity for listening or reasoning of any kind.

Such extreme hunger leaves people psychologically devastated. It strips them of the will to live. Loss of hearing, speech impairment, blindness, difficulty in walking, abnormal heart rhythm and erosion of bone mineral are only a few of the side effects that sustained malnourishment brings.[12]

5. Supporting indigenous churches and Christ groups. If the goal is to facilitate maximum conversions within a country that does welcome missionaries, we must empower local Christians and keep them in charge. In restricted-access people groups, Special Envoys won't have much success at bringing others to Christ without a willingness to work within the local organization of believers, in the spirit of sharing and mutual support.

This cooperation with the local church (if one exists) often can magnify tremendously the Special Envoy's effectiveness. A good example of this is related by Greg Johnson, a missionary of Christian Missionary Fellowship serving among Kenya's Maasai people. Attempting to coordinate relief aid during a recent Kenyan drought, Greg approached church elders in the Koyiaki group area inhabited by the Maasai. "I am only one person," Greg said. "I cannot possibly feed all of Maasailand or even the ten thousand inhabitants within this group."

After some time the elders worked with Greg to coordinate a program that would reach ten thousand people within a geographic area of approximately sixty by forty kilometers. Church leaders listed all the inhabitants, distributed the food, and decided on the "food for work" projects that would be undertaken. One of these involved using people to haul water, mix mud and plaster the walls of a church building being constructed. In other areas, they helped to build an airstrip and constructed cattle dips and roads.

"The church assumed the responsibility, gave of itself untiringly, and worked with the overall committees involved in the appropriate Maasai way," Greg reports. In the process, thousands of people were helped, and the prestige and outreach of the indigenous church to the Maasai was greatly strengthened.

Special Envoys can place great confidence in national Christians, even in countries where Christian activities are severely restricted. These believers often will engage in exceptionally high levels of personal sacrifice for the sake of God's work.

In *God's Smuggler* Brother Andrew tells about Abraham, a Bulgarian peasant Christian. Abraham earned the nickname "Giant Killer" because "he was always setting out to find his 'Goliath'—some high-ranking party official or army man to whom he could bring his witness. On the many occasions when the Goliath won, Abraham ended up in jail. But on the others, when Abraham won, a new soul was added to Christ's church."

Abraham and his wife lived on wild berries and fruit and a little bread, because their unyielding witness had prompted the officials to strip away almost all their means of support. The lesson from Abraham for Special Envoys is simply this: never underestimate the willingness of the national population truly to martyr themselves for Christ.[13]

6. Leaving in time. In development work, we can't stay on the scene so long that we build unnecessary dependency. Usually when development work begins, objectives are set along with a timetable specifying completion dates. This is another reason it's so essential to train disciples who can continue the evangelization after the Special Envoys leave.

Sometimes, of course, the moment of departure isn't a matter of choice and comes sooner than desired. One veteran missionary (really a Special Envoy without the title) worked to make converts within a remote tribe. When the country went Communist, he was forced out. Ten years later he was finally able to return, and he made inquiries about one of the most promising disciples from the period before the revolution. Almost miraculously, he located the young man, who traveled days on foot to rejoin his mentor. As of this writing, the disciple and the missionary are once again working together, reuniting a partnership for Christ.

When the young man eventually rejoins his tribe, they will most likely have a powerful witness from one of their own, in an area of the world that is unreached by the gospel and almost inaccessible to outsiders.

The missionary's patience as he endured a decade-long wait illustrates an appropriate Special Envoy response to a certain fact: in the kinds of populations Special Envoys will encounter, severe and usually unpredictable change will be commonplace. Sudden shifts in population, staff illness and failure, and major alterations in the regulations are to be expected as routine. Special Envoys must therefore become skilled at compensating for such change.

On September 8, 1981, when the Shikhiu refugee camp in Thailand became a detention center, relief workers who had been working with that population suddenly discovered that their presence was barred. Using the seven years' rapport they had previously established with the commander, however, the workers moved cautiously and received unofficial permission to make monthly visits and monthly supply drop-offs.

Similarly, at Thailand's Na Pho refugee camp, long-term workers also found themselves barred. In this case a Thai disciple was chosen to carry on their work, unofficially of course. Because the disciple had been well trained and "fit it" so well, he was actually allowed to conduct a Bible-teaching program in the camp during his regular visits.

Battling with the frequent change and almost constant frustration of such ministries "exposes us to the utter darkness, the appalling madness of man in rebellion against God," reports veteran Christian relief and development worker Cliff Westergren. It also underlines "the necessity of the Christian answer which is outside of man and goes to the core of his need."[14]

7. *Visible prayer-centeredness.* Even in a very restricted country, the Special Envoys, as foreigners, will usually be allowed to pray publicly and practice their personal religious beliefs, at least to a point. So if we wish unbelievers to trust in the efficacy of prayer, we must demonstrate by our actions the level of our faith in prayer and the loving nature of the Lord. Even when we can't tell them what we believe, we can certainly show them. And we must.

In the mission field it often will be essential for Special Envoys to conduct their personal prayer life at a higher level of visibility than they might prefer if back at home. Miriam Adeney tells of a missionary serving a Latin American tribe who discovered that the Christian converts among the tribe had held a prayer meeting for a sick member but had not invited him.

Distressed at not being included, the missionary asked why. The answer: "We didn't know whether you really believe God can heal." When faced with sickness or injury, he realized that the villagers had seen him offering pharmaceutical help, rather than prayer.

Adeney continues, "A Muslim prays five times a day, wherever he is. A pagan prays before he plants a field, before he harvests, before he builds a house. When we go to other countries, we must stop our Western compartmentalizing of the secular and the sacred." Adeney recommends that office personnel in foreign countries learn to stop and pray with colleagues in the middle of managerial problems, and agriculturists learn to stand and pray in the middle of fields. In short, Special Envoys need to adopt a religious style that makes sense within the culture in which they are attempting to minister.[15]

8. *No strings attached.* By using conversion as a precondition for aid, we lose credibility as servants of the Lord, who loves all people equally. It will probably also mean getting thrown out of the country, and deservedly so.

In fact, in a relief situation we must not even think about evangelism until the real disaster phase is ended. The goal is to demonstrate God's enduring love, not opportunism. Our best opportunity for witness during the disaster and its immediate aftermath will be our actions: serving the suffering selflessly and turning to God faithfully—and visibly—for the energy and support that we will surely need.

Actions rather than words must always be a beginning principle for the Special Envoy who wishes to succeed in the Third World. Especially in less-developed areas, Envoys will need to be willing to invest a lot of themselves in the process.

Miriam Adeney describes the case of Bruce Olson, a medical worker with the Motilones of the South American jungles. When Olson first tried to introduce simple modern medicines to these people, they refused to use them. Then one day an epidemic of pinkeye swept through the village. Soon everybody had burning, running eyes. Olson had a simple antibiotic that would tackle the disease, but the people wouldn't use it. In desperation, he finally exposed himself to pinkeye and went to the native healer, asking her assistance. "Bruce, I wish I could help you," she answered, "But I've tried every herb and chant I know. Nothing works. I'm worn out."

Olson then pulled a tube of ointment out of his own pocket. "Well, Auntie, I do have some white man's medicine. I wonder if you would be willing to smear some on my eyes." She complied. Bruce was cured, and the native healer tried the same medicine on all the others who were afflicted—with, of course, the same result.

Because of Olson's willingness to risk his own health and to empower the native healer, she began to listen to his suggestions. The same spirit of self-sacrifice and a willingness to work through the native channels will be an essential technique for all Special Envoys.[16]

9. Cooperation. It is imperative in relief and development to demonstrate the highest level of cooperation within the body of Christ. Fortunately, this cooperation comes much easier in the field, especially in a restricted country or people group where all Christian development workers are more or less on their guard and at risk.

One case of such cooperation has occurred in Nepal, where Christian professionals have been at the forefront of that country's entrance into the twentieth century. "In a land that knew no Christians only three decades ago, today there are thousands of believers in hundreds of worshiping communities all across Nepal—'a closed country with an open heart.' "[17]

Art Beals ascribes much of this success to the combined efforts of Christian professionals (much like Special Envoys) from more than thirty countries, who together constitute the United Mission to Nepal. Through their efforts, Beals says, "hydroelectric dams, bridges and roads . . . agricultural and community health programs, plywood mills and furniture factories"—all have been used to "announce the loving presence of Jesus Christ."[18]

As a result of these symbiotic ministries, the people's needs—both physical and spiritual—have been met, and the harvest for Christ has been both profound and enduring.

10. Linking up with radio. It's not always possible, but where it is, Special Envoys can increase their effectiveness by working in concert with a native-language Christian broadcast ministry that reaches the Envoys' target population, both in situations of great physical need and elsewhere.

By working together, radio broadcasters and God's Special

Envoys can penetrate highly resistive countries and people groups more effectively to extend the church of Jesus Christ. These two types of specialized ministries together hold a key to reaching the physically and spiritually hungry in restricted countries. This is one of the most critical arenas in world evangelization today. Creative experiments are in order so that new and effective strategies will emerge. Four steps may be taken in such a joint enterprise.

First, test the team's compatibility. Naturally, both broadcasters and Special Envoys must agree on the basic issues that "man does not live on bread alone" (Deut 8:3) and that people without Christ are lost and in need of salvation. In a similar vein, broadcasters must regard their ministry as incomplete if it does not speak to the heartfelt needs of the listeners in a culturally appropriate way. Though functionally varied, the members of the broadcast/Special Envoy team must share compatibility of purpose.

Second, select a target group. Within the world of the unreached are 5,310 different people groups, each distinguished from every other by its special combination of language and ethnicity. Research is primary for selecting a people group, or groups, that will be a receptive target for the combination of personal evangelism and broadcasts. Each people group selected for this combined approach should meet the following criteria: be otherwise very difficult to reach; comprise at least 100,000 people; be in genuine need of development assistance; and contain a Christward movement in a fairly large section of its population (perhaps 2 or 3 percent of the population).

The physical needs of the chosen groups should be such that the development-trained Special Envoy can be utilized, and that a ten- to fifteen-year commitment can be made for this collaborative ministry. Here, meeting the physical need does not mean feeding people who are starving to death, but rather developing the ability of the area to grow two to five times as much food. The higher the group's receptivity to the gospel, the better chance it will have to be selected for this experiment.

Third, focus narrowly on the target group. The broadcast programs must be produced with the target people—their heartfelt needs and their unique sociocultural backgrounds—kept uppermost in mind. The broadcasters must concentrate their efforts narrowly on the identified segments of the target people who appear to be the most receptive. The programming must reflect the reality of what is happening in the lives of listeners, as discerned by the Special Envoys who are responsible for staying in constant touch with them. This narrow focus on the target group incorporates into programming (among other things) life stories and happenings in the villages, testimonies by recent converts, as well as accounts of the problems faced and conquered by the new believers.

On occasion, the special Envoys may provide transistor radios to groups in strategic locations.

Fourth, use the indigenous (heart) language of the target people. The broadcasting language must not be the general language of the province, but rather the specific language of the segment of the population that has been targeted for this effort. People use the "language of the heart" for communicating to their loved ones and friends and expressing their most intimate thoughts—including matters related to faith. Thus, to be effective, the broadcasters must use this heart language as well.

As partners in this effort, both the Special Envoys and the broadcasters must be well trained to lead people to Christ and to help organize them into Christ groups.

11. Making use of the work of Bible translators. Substantial progress has been reported this century in making native-language translations of Scripture available to more of the world's people, though a great deal of additional work remains to be done. Special Envoys will benefit greatly as these new translations of Scripture become available. As of mid 1990, according to figures compiled by David Barrett and Todd Johnson, 92 percent of the world's population had potential access to some portion of the

Bible in their mother tongue. Mother-tongue access to the whole Bible, on the other hand, was only available to 85 percent of the world's population.[19]

Looking a little further, however, we see that these availability figures may suggest a rosier picture than in fact exists. To begin with, 29 percent of the world's adults are illiterate, and so could not read the Scripture even if it were handed to them. In addition, there are incalculable (though very large) numbers of non-Christians who are blocked from reading the Bible either by severe antagonism to Christian literature within their own country or simply by lack of funds.

In many cases, Special Envoys will be seeking to reach precisely those people groups where Scripture translations are most scarce—due to illiteracy, poverty, government antagonism or some combination thereof.

The ongoing work of Bible translation ministries in many cases will be vital to the Envoys' ability to reach the unsaved, since the ability to distribute Scripture will be especially effective as a method of outreach in places where the proclamation of the gospel is publicly prohibited.

Well-written tracts in the language of the people will also prove to be very valuable in the Special Envoys' ministry. Typical titles for such tracts might include "Basics of the Christian Faith," "How to Organize a Christ Group," "Christ's Way to the Muslim Heart," "Key Verses for Memory," "Victorious Living" and so on. The tracts must address the issues confronting the people for whom they are written.

12. A reminder again: dependence on prayer. Always worth repeating, though sometimes overlooked, is the vital and indispensable role of prayer in supporting every aspect of the church's global mission. In the King James translation of Luke 10:2 we are told: "Pray ye therefore the Lord of the harvest, that he would send forth labourers into his harvest."

The word "pray" is critical here. In fact prayer—both by Special Envoys in the field and by those who support their global mission—is vital and indispensable at all times. There is no knowing how much closer we might come to fuller obedience to the Great Commission if more of us would include this vital subject in our prayers more often.

13. Playing fair with governmental agencies that want to support relief but not evangelism. Christian relief and development agencies walk a tightrope when it comes to evangelism. Our consciousness as an organization is Christian, but implementation of Christian evangelization must be done *on a personal basis.* We must be certain at all times that all our programs reflect sound development and that we never use funds from governmental and intergovernmental sources to spread the gospel. Only funds received from individual donors and earmarked for this purpose should be used for outreach ministries—and these are best employed in such ways as to strengthen the efforts of local churches.

With careful bookkeeping and scrupulous attention to each donor's intent, we can employ governmental funds in ways that they approve and also pursue the vigorous evangelism that many of our donors specify. As Christians, as good stewards, and as responsible professionals we can do no less.

Questions for Thought and Review
1. Describe the special place of ministries related to physical need in the global mission of the church.
2. Explain how as a Special Envoy you might prepare yourself to deal with the severe and often unpredictable change that one so often must face in the mission field.
3. Explain how broadcast ministries might be used to increase the effectiveness of God's Special Envoys.
4. Explain the significance of prayer to the Special Envoy.
5. Discuss how scrupulously honest bookkeeping can allow a Christian relief and development agency to respond to both physical and spiritual hungers, with full conformance to every donor's intent.

8
The Symbiotic Approach to Relief and Development

A MISSIONARY TO THE TINY VILLAGE OF TUBUU IN NORTHERN Ghana discovered the necessity of a symbiotic ministry in an especially painful way. Howard Brant of SIM had been a missionary to the village, then was called away. Two years later, he discovered that the Christian converts he had left had been wooed away by Muslim missionaries, who also were working in the area. The greater success of the Muslims was not theological at all, Brant learned, but rather was based on the fact that they provided development assistance for their converts, whereas Christian converts had received no physical assistance.

"I determined that day that we must find ways of integrating church planting with development," Brant said. "Development is part of the very necessary process in dealing holistically with people like the Mampursi of northern Ghana. They do not make a dichotomy between their souls and their bodies." Dealing with them simply from the perspective of spiritual need, Brant concluded, did not help them solve the problems they believed were primary.[1]

Clearly, a successful witness for Christ in a setting of human need takes very careful timing and just the right blend of a constantly shifting mixture of these two elements—relief and development, and evangelism. The right mixture depends on the situation, and will change as the relief and development process continues.

For some time now, I have been attempting to develop and refine a model that is appropriately adaptable to changing situations, yet heuristic enough to provide guidance to the Christian relief and development worker in the field. I call this the "Contextual Symbiosis Model." Basically, it suggests that we must always strive for an integration of the evangelism and the relief/development components, and that the proportion of the evangelism must increase as we work our way through the relief and development process.

Within this model—which is expressed visually in a Symbiotic Ministry Matrix (see p. 133)—the relief and development process is conceptualized as having three basic (though often overlapping) steps—or "stages of wholeness"—all leading to a fourth. Similarly, the "focus of assistance" to the individual (or group) is also broken into four steps, modeled after the four stages in the earthly development of Christ (see Lk 2:52).

I want to stress the central importance in our thinking of the fact that the matrix can be applied at the level of the individual. At Food for the Hungry we have always said that though the problem of world hunger is overwhelming, we can combat it— "one person at a time." The Symbiotic Ministry Matrix continues this emphasis on "one person at a time" in its ascending assistance typology: physical, mental, social, spiritual. Similarly there are four ascending stages of wholeness: relief, recovery, development, sustainability. I will shortly explain each of these components. But first, I think a little background might be of help.

Over the past fifty years, the field of development has evolved dramatically. Immediately after World War II, development was defined exclusively in terms of the amount of money needed to reconstruct the infrastructures of countries ravaged in the war. Then, in the chaos of the 1960s, agencies began to realize the necessity of addressing the country's social values, plus the mental and social condition of its residents. Finally, in recent years, more development experts are acknowledging the importance of a spiritual dimension in the relief and development process.

Through this evolution, few usable tools have emerged to help us clearly visualize the symbiotic nature of relief and development programs and the path to success in the physical, mental, social and spiritual realms, as described in Luke 2:52. For our organization, however, the Symbiotic Ministry Matrix is such a tool, and it seems to be working for us very well.

As indicated by the matrix, Christian relief and development must take into account the sustainability of the following four interrelated priorities.

Physical progress indicators (agroeconomic and health), including: food security for the community, defined as "ability to sustain enough food, all of the time, for all the people to live a healthy and active life"; reduced malnutrition and increased immunization for children ages 0-5; accessibility of potable water; surplus of production and/or income savings; and sustainable local accessibility to key resources such as repair parts, seeds, trained health workers, medicine and so forth.

Mental progress indicators (knowledge), including: experimentation with and sharing of new ideas; sustainable availability and use of vocational training and at least primary education.

Social progress indicators (characterized by changing social attitudes and improved social practices), including: local skills continuing to develop without the help of an outside agency; cultural ownership of practices as evidenced by replication; and healthy family and social relationships.

Spiritual progress indicators, including: indigenized/culturally relevant Christian groups established with appropriately trained leaders; local Christian groups involved in evangelism and social ministry; local Christian groups having relationships with the larger body of Christ; widespread evidence of the fruits of the Spirit and contentment; and broken power of evil spirits and vices in individual hearts.

Though more cumbersome than relief and development, we think of the process more completely as the Relief-Recovery-Development-Sustainability continuum (R-R-D-S for short). Its ultimate goal is for the people group (or community within it) to attain self-sufficiency and replication. Getting to this point involves a continuum of activities (R-R-D-S) that can begin and end at several different points on the matrix. Each community will progress within each category at its own rate. Thus the matrix needs to be tailored to fit individual contexts. The four steps toward the goal can be described as follows:

At the Relief stage, the first square of the matrix, lives are in danger within the community. Physical goals will probably be to supply basic needs such as food, water, shelter, health care and sanitation. Mental, social and spiritual goals are in place at this stage, but are lower in priority. These may include learning basic survival skills, seeing attitudes change from despair to hope, helping people realize that the help is coming from God, and generating interest in knowing more about Christ. This stage typically lasts about a year.

As the program moves down the matrix to the second stage, Recovery, the goals for physical progress probably will include restoring people to former levels of agroeconomic and health resources. Mental and social goals will include activities to train community members in health practices, leadership and problem-solving techniques. The community will begin using elementary and primary education, and healthy social relationships will begin to develop. Spiritually, individuals will begin to recognize the distinctiveness of Christian life, evidenced by conversions to Christianity and participation in Bible studies. The recovery process typically lasts one or two years beyond the relief stage.

Moving down the matrix to Development, the third stage, goals for physical progress will be characterized by improvements in food supply, use of potable water, increased household income, improved mother and child health, and disaster preparedness. Mental and social goals will include family participation in good health practices and continued improvement in social relationships, evidenced by groups working together to solve problems. Vocational training may begin to be used more extensively. Spiritually, the fruits of the Spirit will begin to blossom, and there will be extensive evangelism and social ministry within the community conducted by local Christians. Independent churches may be established. Because of the need for heavy individual involvement in the community, the development stage typically lasts three to five years beyond the recovery phase.

Sustainability, the final row in the matrix, represents a standard for which we all need to strive. Admittedly, some communities will never reach the goals enumerated earlier in this stage. In some cases, the best interests of the community will be better served by the agency helping them get as close as possible and then pulling out before dependency is created.

To help achieve sustainability the Christian relief and development organization must work in partnership with those in the community, encouraging them to become active partners in the development process. It must *facilitate* the strengthening of the community development system.[2] Thus God's Special Envoys engaged in relief and development must function as *development facilitators*. The Envoys must also assist indigenous churches to grow proficient in ministering to the two hungers prevalent in their ministry areas.

In the heady process of attempting to work as Christ's servants in bringing others to him, we must always, of course, remember

The Symbiotic Ministry Matrix

Stages of Wholeness	Objective	Focus of Assistance *				Year
		Physical	**Mental**	**Social**	**Spiritual**	
Relief	Preservation of life in disaster and refugee situations	✓				1
Recovery	Restoration to former levels	✓	✓			2 3
Development	Progress beyond former levels	✓	✓	✓		4 5 6 7 8
Sustainability	Self-sufficiency, continuing progress, healthy relationships	✓	✓	✓	✓	9 10 11 12

* "And Jesus grew in wisdom and in stature, and in favor with God and men." (Luke 2:52)
✓ = Stage substantially completed

that the timing of these miraculous moments is God's, and that God's plans are far more vast and more wonderful than our small attempts to be systematic and structured in our mission strategies.

Having said this, I proceed with trepidation to offer a few more suggestions about a workable approach to integrating evangelism into the Relief-Recovery-Development-Sustainability continuum. Naturally, it is assumed that Special Envoys will check and modify these suggestions—through prayerful openness to the urgings of the Holy Spirit at the time the actual evangelization efforts are made.

During the Relief stage, evangelism must usually be very subtle. It is primarily expressed as the Special Envoys display the values of their own faith—through constant prayer and through the level of selfless, loving servanthood that reflects the boundlessly loving nature of our Lord.

The second stage, Recovery, permits better opportunities for spoken evangelism, possibly integrated into lessons on rebuilding and administration of the aid that will help the suffering people get back on their feet again.

Throughout both of these stages the Envoys need to establish their credibility as people who understand and care about those being helped.

In the third stage—Development—Envoys should be aware of the difficult and often painful process of cultural and spiritual reorientation taking place within the new or prospective convert's lifestyle, heart and head. It is hoped that during this stage the Special Envoys will participate in God's divine mystery of conversion. Here it is important for them to remember—especially in foreign cultures—that the little ten-letter word "conversion" expresses an eternally significant process that, especially for the non-Westerner, can result in such an extreme reorientation of values, practices and beliefs that the new convert may find himself or herself completely uprooted from all that is familiar and all that appears to be secure. Just because the Special Envoy believes in the rightness of conversion does not mean that the process will be any less disorienting—at least at the early stages— for the person being saved.

Symbiosis: A Unifying Strategy

Over the last few decades, a global battle has been raging between evangelical churches and conciliar churches (those belonging to councils such as the National Council of Churches and the World Council of Churches). The subject: evangelism versus social action in the church's mission. This battle—sometimes called "The Great Debate in Mission"[3]—is both wasteful and unnecessary.

The solution for both evangelical and conciliar churches is to commit to symbiotic ministry—such as I have described as being practiced by Special Envoys in relief and development contexts. This symbiotic ministry blends evangelism (proclamation of the gospel) and social action (meeting people's physical needs in a nonviolent manner) into a single, integrated and vastly more

effective effort.[4] Through the commitment to a symbiotic ministry, churches or members of churches primarily interested in
carrying out the Great Commission can work productively and
in harmony with churches and church members who wish to
minister to both the spiritually and physically hungry of the
world. In the process, both groups would benefit.

To make this point more clear, let me define *symbiotic ministry*
in more global terms. The term *symbiotic* is the adjective of the
compound *symbiosis,* made up of the Greek prefix *sym,* meaning
interdependence, and the Greek morpheme *bios,* meaning life.
Derived from the field of biology, this word depicts the harmonious living together of two functionally dissimilar organisms in
a way that is beneficial to each other. (This is precisely our goal
for both those who favor evangelism and those who favor social
action.)

Referring to symbiosis in nature, Linsley Gressit says the term
"generally implies a distinct interdependence of two quite different living organisms." Gressit continues, "Symbiosis may be
more strictly applied to relationships that are obligatory in some
sense: one partner being unable to live without the other."[5]

Thus, following this usage of the term, the symbiotic ministry
implies that both evangelism and social action, though *separate*
in function, are *inseparable* in relations and are both *essential* to
the total ministry of Christ's church.

The only form of social action absolutely excluded from this
definition—and which I would personally prefer to exclude
entirely from the church—is social action that sanctions use of
political manipulation or violence. For reasons of both effective
tactics and sound theology, these coercive methods have no
place ever among the strategic approaches used by God's Special
Envoys.

With this single exception, then, I would hope that churches
from different philosophical camps—as well as the Special Envoys they send into the field—might be able to find unity of
purpose as they support ministries that are symbiotic.

I previously provided numerous reasons why evangelistic goals would be better achieved in restricted countries by being joined to social (needs-oriented) ministries that take a genuine symbiotic approach. Let me now outline a few of the benefits to be gained by churches that emphasize social action when they also support symbiotic causes and ministries, and when they lend their support to Special Envoys who will be utilizing a symbiotic approach:

1. *It's biblical.* As the next chapter will show, the symbiotic approach is more consistent with biblical teachings than one which emphasizes only social action goals.

2. *It works better in "enemy" territories.* Purely social-action-oriented ministries tend to get in trouble with repressive administrations because of the frustration of "not being able to change enough without changing the government first." The symbiotic approach, on the other hand, sets individual conversions as the goal, rather than social "reform." The result is that symbiotic ministries—especially as practiced by God's Special Envoys—leave Caesar undisturbed and concentrate on doing God's work.

3. *It avoids parasitism.* Parasitism occurs when "one organism appears to have all the advantages while the other is harmed."[6] Parasitism is often the problem when a more liberal (conciliar) church's ministry gets out of balance, with so much emphasis on the more strident forms of social action that members become dissatisfied and eventually leave the church. In these cases, the first members to leave often tend to be the church's more conservative and more affluent supporters. The solution is support of symbiotic ministries, where the proper balance is intentionally maintained.

4. *It avoids parallelism.* Effective symbiotic ministries, as previously explained, almost never provide a 50-50 balance of evangelism and social action (relief/development). In properly managed symbiotic ministries, the balancing of these components takes place in the field and is adjusted in accordance with the situation and the promptings of the Holy Spirit to achieve

optimum mission results. The risk of keeping evangelism and social action separate (that is, nonsymbiotic) is that the balancing often takes place in the church's budgeting process and usually results in a rigid 50-50 mixture, which never seems to fit exactly the needs of the field.

Before we go on to review how the Special Envoy strategy is consistent with God's plan revealed through Scripture, I close with another illustration of symbiotic ministry at work.

In the hill country of North India, a region containing some fifty thousand villages was known for a high incidence of tuberculosis and other endemic diseases. In 1983 a program was begun to bring primary health care to these villages. Working together with the Evangelical Alliance Mission (TEAM) to develop the three-year pilot project was Dr. Barry Mackey, who was then West Asian director of World Relief. Dr. Mackey's goals were to reduce the incidence of the endemic diseases, to curb malnutrition and to provide trained medical workers in several selected villages.

Jerry Ballard, then executive director of World Relief, comments on his visit to this area two years later:

Not only did I find clinics well-established in the six project villages with trained local staff, I found six Christian groups meeting regularly for worship and Bible study.

It seems that professional excellence, the demonstration of the reality of our Christian faith through action, and our personal witness to the power of the gospel must all find a rightful place in a definition of Christian compassionate ministry, whether we call it relief and recovery, development, or whatever. As Christians we would do well in the midst of much needed social action to remember the words of our Lord, "What shall it profit a man, if he shall gain the whole world, and lose his own soul?"

Whether it be refugee camps in Southeast Asia, famine relief and development assistance in Africa, working with dislocated peoples in Central America, or wherever God's people have gotten involved—really involved—in the lives of people around them, God has used His people to provide both help for the body and hope for the soul.

Through our integrated relationship with the churches, we've seen closed towns and villages opened to the gospel and the church planted on every continent as the direct result of faithful stewardship of both our physical and spiritual resources.[7]

Questions for Thought and Review

1. Explain the principle of contextual symbiosis.
2. Explain why symbiosis can be seen as a "unifying strategy."

9
The Special Envoys' Mandate in Scripture

To become one of God's special envoys is to make a major commitment of service to the Lord. There will be risks. There will be loneliness. There will be much hard work.

Certainly those who are contemplating this vocation should be convinced that the style and the strategies of the Special Envoys are consistent with God's plan. As Christians, our best resource for making such a determination is, of course, the Bible. In this chapter are various biblical references for your study. Looking at these should be combined with a scriptural exploration of your own, plus something else: the urgings of the Holy Spirit, revealed through prayer.

Earlier we have seen some of the basic scriptural support for the vocation, the style and the strategies of the Special Envoys. We discussed also the church's biblical mandate for the global mission, and listed passages indicating the consistency with which the Bible instructs us to provide for those in need. Now we will briefly review the biblical basis for some of the other aspects of the Special Envoys' mission and approach.

Models for Symbiotic Ministries

Beginning with the New Testament, we see in the life of Jesus a symbiotic ministry in action. Throughout the Synoptic Gospels (Matthew, Mark and Luke) we find Jesus teaching, preaching and healing—that is, ministering to both physical and spiritual needs. Matthew describes the Lord's ministry this way: "Jesus went throughout Galilee, teaching in their synagogues, preaching the good news of the kingdom, and healing every disease and sickness among the people" (Mt 4:23). Teaching, preaching and healing were treated as separate functions, but were all essential components of the total, integrated ministry of Jesus.

The very definition of the church as "the body of Christ" attests to the correctness of a symbiotic ministry—in which functionally separate elements work in coordination to carry out God's plan. In his epistles to the Romans and to the Corinthians, the apostle Paul defines the church as the body of Christ, consisting of diverse members, each with its own function, but all working symbiotically. "Just as each of us has one body with many members, and these members do not all have the same function, so in Christ we who are many form one body, and each member belongs to all the others" (Rom 12:4-5).

Elsewhere, speaking of the ministry Christ intends for his church, Paul says,

It was he who gave some to be apostles, some to be prophets, some to be evangelists, and some to be pastors and teachers, to prepare God's people for works of service, so that the body of Christ may be built up until we all reach unity in the faith and in the knowledge of the Son of God and become mature, attaining to the whole measure of the fullness of Christ. (Eph 4:11-13)

The life of the early church as reported in the book of Acts was symbiotic ministry in action. In the early stages of the church's life following Pentecost, Christians were engaged in both proclaiming the good news (evangelism) and meeting each other's needs (the social ministry).

Thinking further about Paul's depiction of the church as a body, we see the scriptural basis for another characteristic of the Special Envoys—one that frequently accompanies their symbiotic ministry. This characteristic is that they are not "Lone Rangers," disconnected and, in the current secular phrase, "doing their own thing." Rather they work cooperatively with others whenever possible. Or, more precisely, they work *synergistically*.

Synergism is the special cooperative state that is achieved when "discrete agencies" (people, relief organizations and so forth) interact in such a way "that the total effect is greater than the sum of the individual effects."[1] The cooperation between Special Envoys and broadcast ministries (see chapter seven) is an example of synergism. So is the cooperation between Special Envoys and Bible translators, or the cooperation between Envoys and members of the local church.

In fact, one can see our current, global effort to reach the remaining unreached peoples as a wonderful opportunity for synergism on an enormous scale. All that is required is the willingness to cooperate, a mutual respect among the participants and a shared understanding of the mission.

In business circles these last few years, the advocacy of synergism and synergistic management has become very popular.[2] What is interesting about this new popularity is that perhaps the best example of synergism took place nearly two thousand years ago—in the inspired cooperation of the early church (Acts 1—28).

Contextual Symbiosis

In the New Testament, we note not only that the ministries are synergistic and symbiotic, but that they are symbiotic in accordance with contextual factors. We see this principle of contextual symbiosis first of all in the life of Jesus, who varied the nature and type of his ministry to fit the situation. For example, in ministering to members of the upper classes such as Sadducees, Pharisees, lawyers and scribes, his ministry was primarily that of preaching and theological discourses. With these groups he was rarely involved in healing or feeding.

In his ministry to the masses, on the other hand, Jesus' approach included not only preaching and teaching but also healing and feeding. And in still other contexts, such as his encounter with a Syro-Phoenician woman, his ministry was primarily one of healing.

In these cases, the nature of the needs and the audience was the determining factor (just as it will be for God's Special Envoys). In sending forth the Twelve into a preaching and healing mission (Mt 10), Jesus instructed them to let their movement be guided by the nature of people's receptivity to them.

Not surprisingly, the early church's symbiotic ministry was also tailored to fit differing contexts. As long as the church remained predominantly Jewish, it expressed its faith and life largely in traditional Jewish ways, such as worshiping in the temple and practicing circumcision. When the church moved into the Gentile world, the new context called for the different expression of faith and life that now is known as "Paul's strategy for the Gentiles."[3]

Old Testament Origins

As is usual with so many biblical themes, the principles of symbiosis and contextual symbiosis that are so conspicuous in the New Testament were actually outgrowths of earlier Jewish practices that began centuries before. If we take the Old Testament traditions seriously, we note that in the earliest stage of Israel's life as God's people two distinct forms of ministry emerged: a judicial-prophetic ministry represented by Moses, and a priestly ministry represented by Aaron. These two forms fit our definition for symbiotic ministry. They were functionally separate, but relationally inseparable, and both clearly were essential to the ongoing process of Israel's total life as a covenant community.

The Deuteronomic history fits this pattern as well. It recognized three distinct forms of ministry in the person of Samuel: Samuel as judge, Samuel as prophet, and Samuel as priest. These three offices were functionally separate and yet formed the perspective of Israel's life. They were also in symbiotic relationship, with each office functioning separately but at the same time in unison with the others for the enhancement of Israel's total life as God's covenant community.

Later, the prophetic tradition—especially beginning with Amos—bore witness to the dynamic vitality of symbiotic ministry in the twofold concerns of Israel's prophets: on the one hand, concern for one's vertical, personal relationship with God (or "the knowledge of God," to borrow Hosea's phrase); and on the other hand, concern for one's horizontal relationship ("Learn to do good, seek justice, correct oppression, defend the fatherless, plead for the widow," to borrow Isaiah's words [1:17 RSV]).

From the perspective of the prophets, we have an intimate, personal, loving relationship vertically with Yahweh, and with him alone. In the Hoseanic sense of *da'at elohim,* this vertical knowledge of God was one facet of Israel's covenant responsibility. Another was to "let justice roll down like waters, and righteousness like an ever-flowing stream" (Amos 5:24 RSV) in one's horizontal relationships.

To the prophets, the two were neither identical nor exclusive. They viewed the two relationships (loving God and loving one's neighbor) as involving two distinctly separate objects, but at the same time as mutually inseparable and as both essential for the total life and full realization of God's kingdom. One without the other was insufficient, and a "vain offering," in the words of Isaiah.

Biblical Models for Other Characteristics of Envoys

1. Commitment. Our model for the total, full-life commitment of the Special Envoys is, of course, our Lord himself. As it is so perfectly expressed in 1 John 3:16-18,

> This is how we know what love is: Jesus Christ laid down his life for us. And we ought to lay down our lives for our brothers. If anyone has material possessions and sees his brother in need but has no pity on him, how can the love of God be in him? . . . Let us not love with words or tongue but with actions and in truth.

Likewise we can be confident of his commitment to us. Our Lord's own instructions say: "Come, follow me . . . and I will make you fishers of men" (Mk 1:17) and "Peace be with you! As the Father has sent me, I am sending you" (Jn 20:21).

2. Tentmaking. Paul, the archetypal "tentmaker" missionary, proved conclusively that a full-time ministry is in no way diminished by the decision to support oneself with a full-time job.

In the seventeenth century, the Moravians began their longstanding tradition of bringing people to Christ by employing missionaries who were potters, carpenters, bakers, watchmakers and businessmen.

Two centuries later, William Carey, the "father of modern missions," supported his missionary efforts in India as a shoemaker. "My business is to witness for Christ," he said. "I make shoes just to pay the expenses."[4]

3. Nonhierarchical structure. Just as in the early church, the Special Envoys will belong to a structure that is without centralized administration. Their unity will come from a common commitment to the Lord and to doing God's will. Their "procedural manual" will be Scripture. Their "organization" will come from their unity of purpose and the dictates of the Holy Spirit.

If all of this seems loose and disorganized, I would suggest that it is no more so than was the early church—which expanded and flourished with precisely this kind of loose structure for centuries. (This nonhierarchical structure was also helpful in producing the synergism of the early church, which achieved an effectiveness far greater than the combined effects of all of the humans who built it.)

4. Empowerment. God's Special Envoys, like the apostles, will need to empower those they help to convert, teaching them to trust in God and in themselves, teaching them to work independently and to empower those whom they bring to the Lord. The willingness and ability to empower others was a prominent characteristic of Paul and the other church planters (Acts 1— 28). It needs to characterize the Special Envoys as well.

5. Nonjudgmental approach. In advising Special Envoys to be culturally nonjudgmental in their approach, I look for authority to Paul's epistles: "Therefore let us stop passing judgment on one another. Instead, make up your mind not to put any stumbling block or obstacle in your brother's way" (Rom 14:13); "Be kind and compassionate to one another, forgiving each other, just as in Christ God forgave you" (Eph 4:32).

Repeatedly in the Scriptures we are told to love one another (for example, Rom 13:8; 1 Pet 1:22; 1 Jn 3:11, 23; 4:7, 11-12; 2 Jn 5). This certainly requires that we not judge.

6. Nonsyncretism. While attempting to bring the unsaved to the Lord, the Special Envoy will need to be nonjudgmental about those cultural beliefs which are not inconsistent with explicit biblical teaching. On the other hand, the Envoy must never shun the responsibility to point these people toward God—and away from false religion. There is no room for vacillation here.

Elijah expressed this need to make a clear and firm decision many centuries ago: "How long will you waver between two opinions? If the Lord is God, follow him; but if Baal is God, follow him" (1 Kings 18:21).

In conclusion: We have an unchanging mandate and an unchanging Lord. Clearly, the biblical roots go deep for the Special Envoys charged to do his work.

Questions for Thought and Review

1. Who and what are the scriptural models for the symbiotic ministries?

2. Where is the principle of contextual symbiosis revealed in the Old Testament? Where in the New Testament?

3. In what other ways does Scripture support the ministry of God's Special Envoys?

PART 4
Taking the First Step

10
How to Get Started

By NOW YOU HAVE READ THE REQUIREMENTS FOR BECOMING one of God's Special Envoys. You've learned about the training they should undergo and the insights that will prepare them to work effectively. You've also looked in on a few of these Special Envoys in action—battling fierce obstacles and prevailing in Jesus' name to bring some of the unreached to the one true Way.

Perhaps you're beginning to feel a quiet but steady pressure within to get more involved. Maybe the Holy Spirit is speaking to you right now. If so, it is important to respond. From the stories of others who have become involved in mission work, we learn that the initial inner urgings often seemed very subtle, hard to discern. In fact, for most of us, the message really doesn't become clear until we act. It is the process of taking action in response to the Holy Spirit's urging that often provides the real clarity. Without responding, you'll probably never know.

Remember Paul on the road to Damascus? Surely his vision when the Lord Jesus appeared to him was among the strongest of heavenly proddings. Yet his ministry didn't begin until he received further confirmation through the loss of his eyesight and its subsequent restoration by God through the hands of Ananias (Acts 9:3-19).

Remember also Gideon, whom God instructed to go and save Israel from the mighty army of the Midianites, the first people known to use camels in battle (Judges 6:14). " 'But, Lord,' Gideon asked, 'how can I save Israel? My clan is the weakest in Manasseh, and I am the least in my family' " (Judges 6:15). Gideon obeyed God's command, but not until he had been lavishly reassured that the message was legitimate and the Lord's promises real. Before Gideon finally moved into action, God had encouraged him with the miracle of fire emerging from a rock (Judges 6:19-21), and with two additional miracles involving a fleece and dew on the ground (Judges 6:36-40).

If your calling to be a Special Envoy is genuine, you will surely be confirmed in this calling. But those miracles are likely to come only after you have moved to action.

Establishing Your Spiritual Support

A first step of response would be to speak to your pastor or minister and ask for encouragement and prayer support. If at all possible, you might also seek a public dedication, possibly in an altar call at your church or in a Bible study group to which you belong.

Support through the prayers and concern of your fellow Christians is vital—especially at these early stages—as your commitment to a crosscultural ministry grows. One reason for this is that the Special Envoy identity is not (as we all know) in keeping with the norms of the secular culture. You thus need to be regularly embedded in a small, supportive, Christian group that *does* value that role. And by publicly identifying yourself as a Special Envoy (or Special Envoy trainee) within your Bible study or prayer group, you strengthen yourself in that role, and make it powerful within yourself.

Recent research on blood donors in various countries has shown that the people who give blood month after month and year after year tend to be those who have friends who also engage in this kind of self-sacrificial helping behavior.[1] Being one of God's Special Envoys is also self-sacrificial helping behavior. And, similarly, you will need to surround yourself with supportive others who acknowledge and value you in that role, especially at the beginning when the new identity is still taking root.

If one-on-one, personal evangelism is not yet a habit with you, another finding from the research may be of help. This stresses the importance of repeating this initially somewhat intimidating behavior—making it habitual, repeating it often, especially at the start, until you see it as a natural and rewarding expression of yourself.[2] To be sure, one-on-one evangelism is one of the most joyous expressions imaginable of our connection to the Lord. But no one can truly know this joy in witnessing without practicing it often enough to gain confidence, a style that is "you," and to accumulate ample experiences of the life-changing joy that your witness can bring to others.

This will also be the time to start seeking more educational preparation, as described in chapter five. In chapter twelve you'll find a suggested list of educational institutions. The course you choose will depend on many factors, including your age, your educational level, your family status and whether you are already located in or near the unreached people group in which you plan to serve.

As you prepare for the Special Envoy calling, you might wish to seek the support of traditional missionary organizations. Or perhaps you will turn to a worshiping body such as your church. Although this book has attempted to provide guidance in these matters, you will have to work out these decisions yourself through regular prayer and careful listening to God's unfolding plan for you.

After training, when your calling is both tested and clarified, you may wish to be commissioned through a special service at your church or through a particular missionary organization. Even if you elect to be a tentmaker missionary who will be financially self-supporting, you should never endeavor to go without the support of friendship, concern and prayer that a body of fellow Christians can best provide. (Naturally, if your ministry is to a certain gospel-resistant region, you will also want to make provisions so that the expressions of this support do not place you at risk.)

Being "sent" to your mission field by the church where you worship has a number of great advantages, even though the sending will most likely involve neither financial nor administrative support. First, you gain confidence and strength in your calling through a public proclamation of your intent. Second, you receive a commitment for prayer support by those who will be witnessing your commissioning. This will also be the community that you can "report to" from time to time during the course of your service. Finally, by standing in front of a group of fellow Christians and proclaiming your desire to serve as a Special Envoy, you will be witnessing to a kind of commitment that may provide encouragement to others.

Placement in the Field

One way of becoming a Special Envoy is already to have employment in an unreached people group. In this case your "becoming" is simply to recognize and provide a name for the role you already occupy. As previously discussed, you can then secure additional training and begin practicing this role, until it becomes fully a part of you.

Another and more common situation will be first to identify a country or people group where your skills will be valued. You can then tailor your training to the exact context within which you plan to work.

Remember that God's Special Envoys can earn their living in

a wide variety of ways. The apostle Paul was a tentmaker. William Carey made shoes. Other options can be virtually any morally righteous profession that will be of value in your chosen people group and that will be valued enough by its government so you can gain access to the country.

To help you find an appropriate area for service, appendix B provides a list of all 145 countries that have unreached people groups. This list is organized by region, with those regions much higher in spiritual and physical needs listed first. Within this listing is the latest data on numbers of non-Christians in each country and numbers of unreached people groups predominantly located in each. There are also six regional maps, again locating the unreached people groups.

If additional help is required, you will find some references— books to read, people to contact—in chapter twelve. You will also be able to receive guidance and support from many missionary organizations. In addition, one reason for stating publicly in your church your intent to be a Special Envoy is that this will draw out other church members who may have suggestions or contacts that can help you.

Some readers of this book will already have many glorious accomplishments for Christ to their credit. But others have none, and it is my hope that they will be moved to embark on this most wonderful of human experiences for the first time.

If you have never had the experience of bringing others to Christ, you will surely need to seek training in this endeavor. There is a rich body of knowledge available for this purpose, which can vastly improve your skills. Some of it is probably to be found in the library of your church. Other resources are identified in chapter twelve and the bibliography at the end of this book.

If you are about to be a first-time evangelist, you no doubt will feel some discomfort, and perhaps misgivings as well. To be successful at evangelization, it helps to have a good teacher. It is hoped that such a teacher will be available through your own church. In a few denominations, however, evangelistic skills are not so highly prized. If you are in one of those denominations, don't despair. You're in a wonderful position to create a bridge between your denomination and some of the more evangelical churches. I would suggest that you contact the pastor of one of those churches and ask for the training you need. The pastor will be pleased to assist, and you will be helping to bring about a great unity within the body of Christ.

Your single most important step will simply be to begin—to witness to others about Christ. Part of the great surprise in store for you will be the numbers of people who will be overjoyed at what you are offering them. Remember, however, the sad but true fact that our Lord made clear in the parable of the wedding banquet: Though "many are invited . . . few are chosen" (Mt 22:14). A similar message is contained in the parable of the sower in Matthew 13:3-9.

Even when you become an "expert evangelist," it helps to remember that you're only going to succeed in a portion of your evangelization efforts—probably in only one encounter out of many.

A Crosscultural Ministry at Home
As the next step, once you've grown more effective at evangelization with an audience that is culturally familiar to you, you will want to develop skills in working with people from other cultures. Fortunately, with the increased mobility of the international student population, this is getting easier to achieve. In the United States there are estimated now to be more than half a million foreign university students, up from 34,000 thirty-five years ago.[3] Through this contact with foreign students, you may also find yourself guided to the population where you can best carry out your ministry.

Remember too that major cities in much of the industrialized world have growing numbers of immigrants from the Third World, including immigrants from a number of unreached people groups. These too can be ideal target groups for your crosscultural ministry training.

One special benefit of working with foreign students or immigrants to hone your evangelization skills is that you will be able to take advantage of new techniques that recently have been identified and used with great success to reach ethnic groups in the United States. Here are modified versions of these techniques, which prospective Special Envoys might find useful in evangelizing foreign students or immigrants within their own countries:

1. Abandon the notion that the assimilationist approach is the only right way. Current research indicates that the prospect of being assimilated into a dominant group's congregation may not be at all appealing or compelling to members of other ethnic groups. (See the "Measure of Ethnic Consciousness" in chapter six.)

2. Focus on the goal of evangelizing, rather than Americanizing, Westernizing or "civilizing."

3. Accept the heterogeneous nature of persons even within each ethnic group. They are differentiated socioeconomically, often linguistically, generationally and geographically.

4. Utilize the strong ethnic communal ties (friendship and kinship) to the advantage of spreading the gospel.

5. Make use of parachurch organizations for your outreach (for example, home Bible studies and other forms of Christ groups).

6. Attempt to learn and use the indigenous language of your target group.

7. Work, if possible, in partnership with a member of the group you are trying to reach who is already a Christian.

8. Encourage your church to consider special services or special ministries to support your outreach to the particular target group within which you are attempting to evangelize.

9. Take action—perhaps together with your church—to demonstrate your support of the target group. For example, you

might want to make use of one of the group's national holidays to invite some of the group members to get together.

10. Pray that the Holy Spirit will empower you to realize the lostness of every person without Christ and to act decisively to reach some within your ministry group in his name.[4]

Other Ways to Get Started

If you're currently employed in a secular industry, that too may prove to be an excellent training ground for skills to serve you well as a Special Envoy. One advantage of being a "corporate witness" is that you can gain experience witnessing to your professional peers, just as you might be called to do with your coworkers in your Envoy assignment. In addition, the corporate environment will teach you how to witness with discretion, since in almost no cases would you be able to use company time and space for anything other than the most discreet and low-key forms of evangelistic sharing.

Christian ministries may similarly provide opportunities for training that will be of use to you as a Special Envoy. If you choose to work for a Christian relief and development organization, for example, it might be able to provide some on-the-job training that you will need to be skilled in ministering to both spiritual and physical hunger.

Increasingly, however, these organizations require more advance preparation for their staff positions, less so in the area of relief than in development, where increasingly specialized preparation is desired. This is part of what I hope will be a growing trend of higher professional expectations among the "professional Christians" who work in various capacities in Christian ministries.

If we are going to devote our lives to serving the Lord, I believe we should use every bit of skill, talent and education available, so that our service can be of the highest quality and make the maximum contribution to furthering God's kingdom. When the cause is good, the quality of staff and their training needs to be excellent, certainly no less than one would expect in a secular job.

Just as you will be expected to be exemplary in both moral and spiritual development as a Special Envoy, so also should you attain excellence in your passport skill.

Your Special Calling

During this "seasoning period," as you practice and refine your skills for the challenges of a ministry to an unreached people group, you will most assuredly be one of God's envoys—doing his work and contributing to the growth and health of his church. For purposes of clarity, I reserve the title "God's Special Envoys" only for those envoys who are actually at work in an unreached people group. This is not, however, to denigrate the valuable contribution you will make during your training period, as you endeavor to bring others to Christ.

I hope that you will be blessed to conduct your training period amid a supportive Christian community. This will help you move more smoothly through the inevitable maturation process in which you initially will be enthusiastic, then depressed, and finally reach a more realistic understanding of your ministry and what you can expect.

This seasoning period also will provide you with an opportunity to become more attentive to the subtle urgings of the Holy Spirit. As you open up to become more and more trusting in the Lord, you will doubtless find that his leadings are taking you in new directions that may surprise you. Perhaps you will find that your calling is more to be God's envoy to a particular group within your own country, rather than being a Special Envoy to an unreached group.

Many postindustrial nations—like the United States, Germany, Japan, England or France—have an increasing need for specialized ministries to ethnic populations and to disadvantaged groups in urban settings. Within the United States, for example, there is a great need for envoys trained to minister to the many Native Americans who have left the reservation and moved to cities. If you are a citizen of a European country, on the other hand, you might conduct an important evangelistic outreach to followers of Islam, which is now the second largest religion in Europe.

As always, God's plan is much more subtle and far larger than the human mind can grasp. The very process of beginning your preparation to be one of God's Special Envoys will make you a participant in that plan. And if you listen carefully, you will find the Spirit guiding you to greater and greater levels of involvement.

Thus, you must first begin with prayer, then take action, always listening so that you are one with God's purposes. And in the process, the Great Commission will be carried forth.

Early in my career I undertook an extensive study of church growth in Japan, a study that eventually became a book. The bulk of my research was focused on answering one question: "Just how does the church grow in a predominantly non-Christian culture?" There were a number of answers to this question, all of which have in one way or another been shared in this book. One finding, which at first seems so obvious that it is often overlooked, is that those groups which the Lord blesses with the most conversions are the ones that have the most trained missionaries and nationals devoted to the task.

That's a simple finding, but it points directly at us all. If we seriously intend to spread the gospel of our Lord throughout the world, we need large numbers of people who will be committed to that task. This means that none of us can stand idly by and expect the goal to be achieved. We must participate, for by nonparticipation we could keep salvation from those individuals who were possibly ours alone to reach.

Questions for Thought and Review
1. Would you be willing to serve as one of God's Special Envoys?
2. If so, what initial steps must you take? And which of these have you already taken?

11
The Great Adventure Begins

All ABOUT US A WAR IS GOING ON—THE BATTLE FOR THE HEARTS and souls of humankind. Whether we like it or not, we are participants in this war. If we remain on the sidelines, we yield victory to the enemy. The forces of hunger, oppression, ignorance, hatred, death and false religions will have gained sway.

God is not forcing us to join this battle. We live in a free creation. But through our Lord Jesus Christ, he is pointing the way. On one side—nonparticipation—is a less abundant life for ourselves and despair for our brothers and sisters whom we might have helped. On the other side is life at its fullest: life eternal beginning now.

A Time of Decision

As I was beginning to write this chapter, I happened to talk with a friend about another mutual friend. Let us call him Philip.

Philip is one of those individuals who radiates the heart of Christ wherever he goes. He is the kind of person who, in a gospel-resistant country, would provoke the question, "What's different about you? What is it you have that we don't?" As we talked about Philip, my companion mentioned another person in the same profession. He said, "Oh, yes, he's the one who brought Philip to Christ."

I was surprised. Then I thought, "What if he hadn't?" Philip's magnificent witness would not be there to show me the heart of Christ that can be in us all. My friend Philip is a saved and special human being, because one of God's fishermen brought him into the net.

Then I remembered the other Philip who was also brought in, as were Matthew, John, Peter, Thaddaeus and the others. In every case it took a human being acting as an "envoy" of the Father to pass on that spark of salvation—which could then be passed by them to others, who passed it on as well.

We each hold within our heads and hearts the ability to expand God's kingdom to the parts of the world we touch. We can each magnify the purpose of our own lives by passing along that divine understanding of Truth to others.

The company of God's Special Envoys is just one of the units in Christ's mighty army where we might spend our lives, increasing the riches of humankind. However, it is a very special unit that requires an immediate enlistment of 600,000 trained and able workers for our Lord.

Christ's army is the only army in the world in which the soldiers bring life—not death. It is the only army in which those conquered are set free. Likewise, it is the only army strong enough to strip the unspeakable violence from those who use terrorism and death to achieve their ends.

Within us all, I am convinced, there is a deep need to make a contribution to good. There is a need to bring hope where there is darkness now—to bring life where all around we see the encroachment of death. This need can be met by being one of God's Special Envoys.

The Priceless Rewards

As a Special Envoy in an unreached people group, one can achieve unmatched, unequaled experiences of the power of Christ. Even in more open lands you will see the miracles of redemption and rebirth unfold again and again before your eyes. Some of this majesty of Christ's church in a restrictive country is revealed through Carl Lawrence's stories, collected from persecuted Christians in China. Other examples exist in the witness of Brother Andrew and in the inspiring stories of Christian political prisoners whose lights burned brightly in the frozen desolation of the Gulag Archipelago, that terrifying chain of political prisons that existed in the former Soviet Union.

If you accept this challenge and follow through with your training, and then are placed as a Special Envoy in a difficult land, you will discover for yourself precisely what Carl Lawrence, Brother Andrew and the others are talking about. I can think of no thrill equal to the magnificence of Christian witness in areas where so many are suffering for want of what God's Special Envoys bring.

The church that is battling the darkness is the church that reveals God's will in a very special way. Oh, if I could only share with you the joy I myself have experienced kneeling in prayer with rain-drenched refugees along the Cambodian border! Or walking into one of our outposts in East Africa and hearing new Christians singing "Amazing Grace." I remember the eyes of so many physically impoverished people I have seen as they begin to learn about the Lord. Let me tell you, only as we are able to share the gift of the gospel with the poor and needy do we understand, through their eyes and their excitement, the truly blessed gift Christ has given to us all.

As a child in Japan I used to read the stories of the *ronin,* the masterless warriors who engaged in deeds of bravery with their flashing *katana,* the magnificent long and deadly Japanese swords. In many other parts of the world that same excitement is shared in the stories of the North American cowboy, battling with blazing six-guns and smashing fists. Those stories were thrilling, but there was something missing. What that was became clear as we learned about other heroes. In Japan, the real heroes were the samurai. They were warriors, too, but they had a purpose in life and a master to serve. In America, the greater heroes were the U.S. marshals. They were as fast and as tough as the cowboy, but they served peace, justice and law.

Whether we like it or not, in this creation we are all in the service of some master. Sometimes the master is wealth, sometimes greed, sometimes chaos and evil. As Christians we have the power to choose the one Master who provides true freedom and eternal, abundant life. Our Lord Jesus Christ is also the only Master who will be with us always—in our joy and in our deepest travail.

As Christians we have already accepted the Master in one sense. But there is another level of acceptance that comes as we move forward in his army and dedicate our lives and activities to service for him. This is when the greatest miracles begin. This is when Christ's presence before us and within us intensifies and multiplies, and becomes a constant part of our being.

Dream with me of the day when "the LORD shall be King over all the earth," of that day when "his feet will stand on the Mount of Olives," and "living waters shall flow from Jerusalem" (Zech 14:9, 4, 8 NKJV).

Then, if you will, stand with the disciples, the apostles and all those thousands of brave missionaries who have gone before and are working now to spread the kingdom of God to "every tribe and language and people and nation" (Rev 5:9).

If you take action now, you can reach some of those who may be able to respond only to the special gifts our Lord has given to you alone. And through those you reach, others will be saved. And through them, many more.

As of 1995, there will be an estimated four billion human beings throughout the world who have not yet been led to the only true Way.[1] Of these, nearly 80 percent[2] will live in the 10/40 window countries, which will be the special target of the Special

Envoys, since these countries are so typically home to hunger that is both spiritual and physical. For these two-hunger countries in the 10/40 window, and for the other two-hunger unreached peoples in other parts of the world, God's Special Envoys are the best source of hope.

These unreached have waited so long to hear the gospel. And with their painful combination of spiritual and physical hunger, they are ripe for those Special Envoys who are trained to penetrate the barriers surrounding them—bridging missions' final frontier with the message of love, peace and eternal life.

Let us remember always the world ripe for harvest. The great adventure now before us is to be laborers in God's fields. I pray, and I ask you to join me, that the Lord of the harvest will send out laborers into his harvest, and that perhaps one of those laborers will be you. And I pray that through your participation, "This gospel of the kingdom shall be preached in the whole world for a witness to all the nations, and then the end shall come" (Mt 24:14 NASB).

Amen.

Questions for Thought and Review

1. Explore some of the urgings of the Holy Spirit you have experienced in your own life related to the mission field. You might wish to write these down in order to explore them further. Feel free to keep them to yourself if you wish.

2. Describe how you have responded to these urgings and whether you feel that a further response would be appropriate.

3. Imagine how you might feel if you were a Special Envoy in a country like China or Tunisia right now. Explore some of these feelings in your mind, and try to imagine what your typical day and typical week would be like.

4. Take a moment to pray to ask God's guidance about how you should proceed with the new insights you have gained about yourself and God's plan for you through reading this book.

12
Resources for More Help

In THIS SECTION I TRY TO PRESENT A HELPFUL COMPENDIUM OF resources to assist Special Envoys in getting the training and information that they will need. I have collected these references from highly knowledgeable people and hope that they get you off to a flying start.

Suggested Schools
Once you make the decision to become a Special Envoy, the best solution for your training needs will depend on your situation. If time and funds are available, it would be desirable for all Envoys to be trained within a formal academic setting.

The following lists of suggested institutions include both schools and training programs available in the United States. The original list was prepared primarily by the Lake Wales Consultation Task Force: Doug Millham, World Vision, committee chairperson. I have, however, added to that list and also made a few deletions. The schools listed under "Christian Schools for Crosscultural Training" were either recommended by highly respected sources or were believed noteworthy because of the large number of mission courses they offered. The list entitled "Christian Schools for Relief and Development Training" reflects only those schools which the Task Force had been able to identify as of press time. Those schools listed under "Secular Schools for Relief and Development Training" were recommended by respected professors teaching in that area of study. This list is by no means complete; it had to be shortened due to the large number of such programs available. Listed under "Secular Schools for Training in International Health" are schools that were recommended by specialists in the field and through the literature on missionary medicine.

These lists of suggested schools and training programs are by no means exhaustive and, with one exception, are restricted to institutions in the United States. For prospective Special Envoys residing in other countries, it is hoped that some of these listed institutions can help provide information about resources closer to home.

For more detailed information about educational resources for God's Special Envoys, readers are encouraged to consult Doug Millham's published report on the findings of the Lake Wales Task Force, entitled *Lake Wales Consultation Manual* (Monrovia, Calif.: MARC, 1986).

The list entitled "Christian Schools for Training in Teaching English to Speakers of Other Languages" has been prepared by Dr. Kitty Barnhouse Purgason of Biola University at the request of the author.

Christian Schools for Crosscultural Training

Asbury Theological Seminary
North Lexington
Wilmore, KY 40390
606-858-3581

Biola University
13800 Biola Avenue
La Mirada, CA 90639
310-903-6000

Columbia Bible College
P.O. Box 3122
Columbia, SC 29230
803-754-4100

Dallas Theological Seminary
3909 Swiss Avenue
Dallas, TX 75204
214-824-3094

Denver Seminary
P.O. Box 10,000
Denver, CO 80210
303-761-2482

Fuller Theological Seminary
135 N. Oakland Avevue
Pasadena, CA 91101-1790
818-449-1745

Gordon-Conwell Theological
  Seminary
South Hamilton, MA 01982
508-468-7111

Missionary Internship
P.O. Box 457
Farmington, MI 48024
313-474-9110

Multnomah School
  of the Bible
8435 N. E. Glisan Street
Portland, OR 97220-5898
503-255-0332

Nazarene Theological
  Seminary
1700 E. Meyer Boulevard
Kansas City, MO 64131
816-333-6254

Prairie Bible Institute
Three Hills, Alberta
Canada T0M 2A0
403-443-5511

Southwestern Baptist Theological
  Seminary
P.O. Box 22206
Fort Worth, TX 76122
817-923-1921 Ext. 750

Trinity Evangelical Divinity School
2065 Half Day Road
Deerfield, IL 60015
312-945-8800

U.S. Center for World Mission
1605 Elizabeth Street
Pasadena, CA 91104

Western Conservative Baptist
  Seminary
5511 S.E. Hawthorne Boulevard
Portland, OR 97215
503-233-8561

Wheaton College
HNGR Program
Wheaton, IL 60187
708-752-5199

Other Resources for Crosscultural Training

East-West Center
  Institute of Culture
  & Communication
1777 East-West Road
Honolulu, HI 96848
808-944-7666

SIETAR (Society for Intercultural
  Education Training and Research
1414 2nd St., N.W. Suite 102
Washington, DC 20037
202-296-4710

Stanford Institute for Intercultural
  Communication
P.O. Box A-D
Stanford, CA 94305
415-497-1897

Christian Schools for Relief and Development Training

Eastern College
10 Fairview Drive
St. Davids, PA 19087
215-341-5827

University of the Nations
75-5851 Kuakini Highway
Kailua-Kona, HI 96740
808-326-4454

Goshen College
Division of International
  Education
Goshen, IN 46526
219-533-3161

Warner Southern College
HEART Program
Lake Wales, FL 33853
813-638-1188 or -1426

Wheaton College
HNGR Program
Wheaton, IL 60187
708-752-5199

Loma Linda University
Riverside, CA 92515
714-785-2176

Oral Roberts University
7777 South Lewis Avenue
Tulsa, OK 74171
918-495-6807

William Carey International
  University
1539 East Howard Street
Pasadena, CA 91104
818-797-1200

Regent University
Virginia Beach, VA 23464
8804-523-7400

Secular Schools for Relief and Development Training

University of Arizona
Tucson, AZ 85721
602-621-2211

University of California Los Angeles
African Studies Center
Development Institute
10244 Bunche Hall
Los Angeles, CA 90024

Auburn University
Auburn, AL 36830
205-826-4000

California State University
  Consortium
3801 W. Temple Avenue
Pomona, CA 91768

University of California Riverside
990 University Avenue
Riverside, CA 92521
714-787-1012

Cornell University
International Agriculture
N.Y.S. College of Agriculture
  & Life Science
122 Roberts Hall
Ithaca, NY 14853
607-255-1000

University of Florida
1001 McCarthy Hall
Gainesville, FL 32611
904-392-3261

Virginia Polytechnical Institute
Department of International
  Programs
Blacksburg, VA 24061

Secular Schools for Training in International Health

University of California Los Angeles
Dr. Alfred Newman
School of Public Health,
  Medicine & Nursing
405 Hilgard Avenue
Los Angeles, CA 90024
213-825-5516

University of Hawaii of Manoa
183 Kalakaua Avenue, Suite 700
Honolulu, HI 96815
808-948-8643

Johns Hopkins School of
  Public Health
615 N. Wolfe Street
Baltimore, MD 21205
301-955-5000

Michigan State University
East Lansing, MI 48824
517-355-1855

Tulane University
6823 St. Charles Avenue
New Orleans, LA 70118
504-588-5199

Christian Schools for Training in Teaching English to Speakers of Other Languages

Azusa Pacific University (interdenominational)
Department of International Studies
Azusa, CA
818-812-3434
    Certificate in TESOL (graduate level, 21 units), M.A. in TESOL (36 units),
    M.A. in Language Development (for credentialed teachers, 36 units)

Baylor University
  (Southern Baptist)
School of Education
Waco, TX 817-755-1011
    ESL endorsement (for credentialed teachers, 4 courses)

Biola Univeristy (interdenominational)
Department of TESOL & Applied Linguistics
School of Intercultural Studies
La Mirada, CA
310-903-6000
> TESOL undergraduate minor (19 units), Certificate in TESOL (graduate level, 22 units), M.A. in TESOL (41 units), M.A. in Applied Linguistics (42 units), Supplementary Authorization to teach ESL (for credentialed teachers, 12 units)

Columbia Biblical Seminary and Graduate School of Missions
Columbia, SC
803-754-4100
> M.A. in Intercultural Studies with TEFL Certificate, M.A. in TEFL/ICS (50 quarter units for those with background in Bible, 94 quarter units for those without)

Fresno Pacific College (Mennonite Brethren)
Fresno, CA
209-453-2000
> Certificate in TESOL (graduate level, 18 units), M.A. in Education with an emphasis in Language Development or Bilingual Education (for credentialed teachers, 37 units)

Goshen College (Independent Mennonite)
Goshen, IN
219-535-7000
> TESOL undergraduate minor (20 units)

Grand Canyon University (Southern Baptist)
College of Education
Phoenix, AZ
602-249-3300
> M.A. in Education with an ESL emphasis (for credentialed teachers, 38 units)

Hobe Sound Bible College (interdenominational)
Division of Education
Hobe Sound, FL
407-546-5534
> TESOL undergraduate major (30 units)

Maryland Bible College and Seminary (associated with the
  Greater Grace World Outreach)
Baltimore, MD
410-488-2606
  TEFL Certificate (22 units)

Oral Roberts University (interdenominational)
School of Education
Tulsa, OK
918-495-6518
  M.A. in TESOL (36 units)

Regent University (interdenominational)
School of Education
Norfolk, VA
804-523-7429
  Certificate in TESOL (graduate level, 22-24 quarter units)

Seattle Pacific Univeristy (Methodist)
School of Humanities
Seattle, WA
206-281-2036
  M.A. in TESOL (48 units)

Toccoa Falls College (interdenominational)
Teacher Education Department
Toccoa Falls, GA
404-886-6831
  Three courses at the undergraduate level (6 units)

University of the Nations (associated with Youth with a Mission)
TESOL Department
Kona, HI
808-326-7228
  Summer courses at the undergraduate level (6 units)

Wheaton College (interdenominational)
Graduate School of Missions/Intercultural Studies and Evangelism
Wheaton, IL
708-752-5948
  Certificate in TESL (graduate level, 24 units, stand alone or in conjunction
  with M.A. in Missions/Intercultural Studies); summer courses at advanced
  undergraduate/graduate level (6 units)

William Carey International University (associated with the U.S. Center for
  World Mission)
Pasadena, CA
818-797-1200
  Summer courses at the undergraduate level (5 units)

Other Contacts for Assistance

It is of prime importance that God's Special Envoys be able to
support one another. Though global geography will often make
a physical meeting impossible, it is still essential that mutual
support among Envoys be accomplished in two important ways:
first, through prayer; and second, by sharing research promptly.

In addition, Special Envoys who are already in the field may
wish to consider writing and publishing some of their experiences working in this challenging new area.

Some of the publications that might be interested in these
submissions—or where you might want to read the reports of
other Special Envoys—include the following:

AD 2000 Global Monitor
P.O. Box 129
Rockville, VA 23146

Christianity Today
465 Gundersen Drive
Carol Stream, IL 60188

Church Around the World
Box 220
Wheaton, IL 60189

Evangelical Missions Quarterly
Evangelical Missions Informa-
  tion Service, Inc.
25 W. 560 Geneva Road
Box 794
Wheaton, IL 60187

Global Church Growth
P.O. Box 145
Corunna, IN 46730

International Bulletin of Missionary
  Research
490 Prospect Street
New Haven, CT 06511

International Journal of
  Frontier Missions
7665 Wenda Way
El Paso, TX 79915

Missiology
616 Walnut Avenue
Scottdale, PA 15683-1999

Mission Frontiers
Bulletin of the U.S. Center
  for World Mission
1605 Elizabeth Street
Pasadena, CA 91104

Stewardship Journal
745-C Mountainwood Road
Charlottesville, VA 22903

World Christian
P.O. Box 3278
Ventura, CA 93006

Or, possibly, a publication of your own church or denomination might be interested in your work.

If you choose to submit a manuscript to one of these publications, it is always good practice to retain a copy for yourself. In addition, it is recommended that you include a self-addressed, stamped envelope so the editors can get back in touch with you.

Naturally, you should always attach your name and address, being careful to specify if your name is to be withheld to protect your anonymity in the field. If your mission area is especially sensitive, you may also want to alter some of the names and other details to protect the subjects of your article against persecution.

Articles need not be long. In fact, your chances of publication may be better if the material you send is concisely written and overall quite short.

Additional Helps
If you wish additional information about God's Special Envoys or how you might be more effective as a member of their ranks, please feel free to write to me at either of these addresses:

Food for the Hungry, Inc.
P.O. Box E
Scottsdale, AZ 85252-9987
U.S.A.

Food for the Hungry International
243 Route des Fayards
Case Postale 608
1290 Versoix/Geneva
Switzerland

Food for the Hungry's HUNGER CORPS program also can be a source of direct, hands-on training in crosscultural, Christian relief and development work. Prefield training typically takes four to six weeks. A commitment of three years on the field is required. To learn more about this program, simply complete, stamp and mail the card at the back of this book.

If you're looking for an appropriate mission field and have no other contacts, here are a few resources that can get you started in the right direction.

To get help with opportunities in tentmaking, contact:

Global Opportunities
1594 North Allen, #7
Pasadena, CA 91104

U.S. Association of
  Tentmaking (USAT)
(Dr. John Cragin)
Box 61163
500 W. University
Shawnee, OK 74801

Tentmaker International
  Exchange (TIE)
(John Cox)
Pickenham Ministries
High Beeches, North Pickenham
Swaffham, Norfolk PE37-8J
United Kingdom

A variety of organizations are focusing on the last unreached people groups, some within the 10/40 window, others throughout the world. Nine of these are:

AD 2000 and Beyond Movement
(Luis Bush)
2860 South Circle Drive
Suite 2112
Colorado Springs, CO 80906

AD 2000 Unreached Peoples
  Network
(John D. Robb)
121 East Huntington Drive
Monrovia, CA 91016-3400

Adopt-A-People Clearinghouse
(Frank Kaleb Jansen)
P.O. Box 1795
Colorado Springs, CO 80901-1795

Global Evangelization Movement
(Dr. David B. Barrett)
P.O. Box 129
Rockville, VA 23146

Mission to Unreached Peoples
(Dr. Danny D. Martin)
P.O. Box 45880
Seattle, WA 98145-0880

The Peoples Information
  Network (PIN)
(Dr. Ron Rowland)
7500 W. Camp Wisdom Road
Dallas, TX 75236

The Sentinel Group
(George Otis Jr.)
P.O. Box 6334
Lynnwood, WA 98036

U.S. Center for World
  Mission
(Mobilization Division)
1605 Elizabeth Street
Pasadena, CA 91104

WEC International
(Patrick Johnstone)
Bulstrode, Gerrards Cross
Bucks SL9 8SZ, England

Once you have a certain country or region or people group in mind as a target for your personal ministry, find out as much as possible about the indigenous churches within that target group. This kind of information can be obtained from many of the various sources listed above. Remember that even many highly restricted countries have believers in significant numbers. Where there is a Christian presence, use and support it.

Further information to help you secure employment in a strategic position overseas might come from professional organizations in your vocational area, especially Christian professional organizations. For example, if you are a medical or premedical student or a practicing physician or other health-care worker, you may wish to contact the Christian Medical Society; law students and lawyers could contact the Christian Legal Society, and so on. It would be wise to obtain as much information as possible about overseas work from any professional organization in your field with which you can make contact.

Some of your contacts in your target country, both for professional purposes and for linking up with believers, can come through relationships established with foreign students or immigrants from that country with whom you develop relationships in your home country.

For additional information on the "Hamilton Tentmaker Survey" mentioned at the conclusion of chapter four, contact:

Mr. Don Hamilton, Director
TMQ Research
312 Melcanyon Road
Duarte, CA 91010

In addition to the academic institutions listed on the preceding pages, a helpful, all-purpose contact for assistance would be:

U.S. Center for World Mission
1605 Elizabeth Street
Pasadena, CA 91104

And finally, all those considering overseas mission work are strongly encouraged to attend the Urbana Convention, the largest student mission conference in North America, held every three years in Urbana, Illinois, and organized through another helpful contact:

InterVarsity Christian Fellowship
P.O. Box 7895
Madison, WI 53707-7895

Appendix A:

A Helpful Philosophy: *The Lausanne Covenant*

In this book I have attempted to provide a basic philosophy for God's Special Envoys. I have taken pains that this philosophy be nonrestrictive enough to be incorporated into the belief systems of prospective Envoys from a wide range of Christian backgrounds.

Some will see this freedom from elaborate philosophical boundaries as a blessing. It will permit them, through prayer and scriptural study, to build a philosophical infrastructure that best fits the purposes that the Holy Spirit has ordained for them. Others may desire a more elaborate position statement to which they can respond in developing a philosophy of their own.

For the benefit of this latter group I have received permission to reprint the philosophical position paper that I personally find quite helpful in orienting my own thinking about the mission of the church: the now famous Lausanne Covenant, one of the products of the International Congress on World Evangelization at Lausanne, Switzerland, in July 1974.

There were 2,700 participants from more than 150 nations at the Congress, and more than half of those present came from the Third World. The meeting was reported by *Time* magazine as "a formidable forum, possibly the widest-ranging meeting of Christians ever held."

I hope you will find this covenant helpful as an instrument for refining your own mission thinking. Of particular value is its international and culturally nonjudgmental perspective that, to me, is essential to any who would serve as one of God's Special Envoys.

The Lausanne Covenant
Adopted 1974 by the International Congress on World Evangelization, Lausanne, Switzerland.

Introduction
We, members of the Church of Jesus Christ, from more than 150 nations, participants in the International Congress on World Evangelization at Lausanne, praise God for his great salvation and rejoice in the fellowship he has given us with himself and with each other.

We are deeply stirred by what God is doing in our day, moved to penitence by our failures and challenged by the unfinished task of evangelization.

We believe the Gospel is God's good news for the whole world, and we are determined by his grace to obey Christ's commission to proclaim it to all mankind and to make disciples of every nation. We desire, therefore, to affirm our faith and our resolve, and to make public our covenant.

1. The Purpose of God
We affirm our belief in the one eternal God, Creator and Lord of the world, Father, Son and Holy Spirit, who governs all things according to the purpose of his will. He has been calling out from the world a people for himself, and sending his people back into the world to be his servants and his witnesses, for the extension of his kingdom, the building up of Christ's body, and the glory of his name.

We confess with shame that we have often denied our calling and failed in our mission, by becoming conformed to the world or by withdrawing from it. Yet we rejoice that even when borne by earthen vessels the Gospel is still a precious treasure. To the task of making that treasure known in the power of the Holy Spirit we desire to dedicate ourselves anew.

2. The Authority and Power of the Bible
We affirm the divine inspiration, truthfulness and authority of both Old and New Testament Scriptures in their entirety as the only written Word of God, without error in all that it affirms, and the only infallible rule of faith and practice. We also affirm the power of God's Word to accomplish his purpose of salvation.

The message of the Bible is addressed to all mankind, for God's revelation in Christ and in Scripture is unchangeable. Through it the Holy Spirit still speaks today. He illumines the minds of God's people in every culture to perceive its truth freshly through their own eyes, and thus discloses to the whole church ever more of the many-colored wisdom of God.

3. The Uniqueness and Universality of Christ

We affirm that there is only one Savior and only one Gospel, although there is a wide diversity of evangelistic approaches.

We recognize that all men have some knowledge of God through his general revelation in nature. But we deny that this can save, for men suppress the truth by their unrighteousness. We also reject as derogatory to Christ and the Gospel every kind of syncretism and dialogue which implies that Christ speaks equally through all religions and ideologies. Jesus Christ, being himself the only God-man, who gave himself as the only ransom for sinners, is the only mediator between God and man. There is no other name by which we must be saved.

All men are perishing because of sin, but God loves all men, not wishing that any should perish but that all should repent. Yet those who reject Christ repudiate the joy of salvation and condemn themselves to eternal separation from God. To proclaim Jesus as "the Savior of the world" is not to affirm that all men are either automatically or ultimately saved, still less to affirm that all religions offer salvation in Christ. Rather it is to proclaim God's love for a world of sinners and to invite all men to respond to him as Savior and Lord in the wholehearted personal commitment of repentance and faith.

Jesus Christ has been exalted above every other name; we long for the day when every knee shall bow to him and every tongue shall confess him Lord.

4. The Nature of Evangelism

To evangelize is to spread the good news that Jesus Christ died for our sins and was raised from the dead according to the Scriptures, and that as the reigning Lord he now offers the forgiveness of sins and the liberating gift of the Spirit to all who repent and believe.

Our Christian presence in the world is indispensable to evangelism, and so is that kind of dialogue whose purpose is to listen sensitively in order to understand. But evangelism itself is the proclamation of the historical, biblical Christ as Savior and Lord, with a view to persuading people to come to him personally and so be reconciled to God.

In issuing the Gospel invitation we have no liberty to conceal the cost of discipleship. Jesus still calls all who would follow him to deny themselves, take up their cross, and identify themselves with his new community. The results of evangelism include obedience to Christ, incorporation into his church and responsible service in the world.

5. Christian Social Responsibility

We affirm that God is both the Creator and the Judge of all men. We therefore should share his concern for justice and reconciliation throughout human society and for the liberation of men from every kind of oppression.

Because mankind is made in the image of God, every person, regardless of race, religion, color, culture, class, sex, or age, has an intrinsic dignity because of which he should be respected and served, not exploited. Here too we express penitence both for our neglect and for having sometimes regarded evangelism and social concern as mutually exclusive. Although reconciliation with man is not reconciliation with God, nor is social action evangelism, nor is political liberation salvation, nevertheless we affirm that evangelism and socio-political involvement are both part of our Christian duty. For both are necessary expressions of our doctrines of God and man, our love for our neighbor and our obedience to Jesus Christ.

The message of salvation implies also a message of judgment upon every form of alienation, oppression and discrimination, and we should not be afraid to denounce evil and injustice wherever they exist. When people receive Christ they are born again into his kingdom and must seek not only to exhibit but also to spread its righteousness in the midst of an unrighteous world. The salvation we claim should be transforming us in the totality of our personal and social responsibilities. Faith without works is dead.

6. The Church and Evangelism

We affirm that Christ sends his redeemed people into the world as the Father sent him, and that this calls for a similar deep and costly penetration of the world. We need to break out of our ecclesiastical ghettos and permeate non-Christian society.

In our church's mission of sacrificial service, evangelism is primary. World evangelization requires the whole church to take the whole Gospel to the whole world. The church is at the very center of God's cosmic purpose and is his appointed means of spreading the Gospel. But a church which preaches the Cross must itself be marked by the Cross. It becomes a stumbling block to evangelism when it betrays the Gospel or lacks a living faith in God, a genuine love for people, or scrupulous honesty in all things including promotion and finance.

The church is the community of God's people rather than an institution, and must not be identified with any particular culture, social or political system, or human ideology.

7. Cooperation in Evangelism

We affirm that the church's visible unity in truth is God's purpose. Evangelism also summons us to unity, because our oneness strengthens our witness, just as our disunity undermines our Gospel of reconciliation. We recognize, however, that organizational unity may take many forms and does not necessarily forward evangelism. Yet we who share the same biblical faith should be closely united in fellowship, work and witness.

We confess that our testimony has sometimes been marred by sinful individualism and needless duplication. We pledge ourselves to seek a deeper unity in truth, worship, holiness and mission. We urge the development of regional and functional cooperation for the furtherance of the church's mission, for strategic planning, for mutual encouragement, and for the sharing of resources and experience.

8. Churches in Evangelistic Partnership

We rejoice that a new missionary era has dawned. The dominant role of western missions is fast disappearing. God is raising up from the younger churches a great new resource for world evangelization, and is thus demonstrating that the responsibility to evangelize belongs to the whole body of Christ. All churches should therefore be asking God and themselves what they should be doing both to reach their own area and to send missionaries to other parts of the world. A reevaluation of our missionary responsibility and role should be continuous. Thus a growing partnership of churches will develop and the universal character of Christ's church will be more clearly exhibited.

We also thank God for agencies which labor in Bible translation, theological education, the mass media, Christian literature, evangelism, missions, church renewal and other specialist fields. They too should engage in constant self-examination to evaluate their effectiveness as part of the church's mission.

9. The Urgency of the Evangelistic Task

More than 2,700 million people, which is more than two-thirds of mankind, have yet to be evangelized. We are ashamed that so many have been neglected; it is a standing rebuke to us and to the whole church.

There is now, however, in many parts of the world an unprecedented receptivity to the Lord Jesus Christ. We are convinced that this is the time for churches and parachurch agencies to pray earnestly for the salvation of the unreached and to launch new efforts to achieve world evangelization. A reduction of foreign missionaries and money in an evangelized country may sometimes be necessary to facilitate the national church's growth in self-reliance and to release resources for unevangelized areas. Missionaries should flow ever more freely from and to all six continents in a spirit of humble service. The goal should be, by all available means and at the earliest possible time, that every person will have the opportunity to hear, understand, and receive the good news.

We cannot hope to attain this goal without sacrifice. All of us are shocked by the poverty of millions and disturbed by the injustices which cause it. Those of us who live in affluent circumstances accept our duty to develop a simple lifestyle in order to contribute more generously to both relief and evangelism.

10. Evangelism and Culture

The development of strategies for world evangelization calls for imaginative pioneering methods. Under God, the result will be the rise of churches deeply rooted in Christ and closely related to their culture.

Culture must always be tested and judged by Scripture. Because man is God's creature, some of his culture is rich in beauty and goodness. Because he is fallen, all of it is tainted with sin and some of it is demonic. The Gospel does not presuppose the superiority of any culture to another, but evaluates all cultures according to its own criteria of truth and righteousness, and insists on moral absolutes in every culture.

Missions have all too frequently exported with the Gospel an alien culture, and churches have sometimes been in bondage to culture rather than to Scripture. Christ's evangelists must humbly seek to empty themselves of all but their personal authenticity in order to become the servants of others, and churches must seek to transform and enrich culture, all for the glory of God.

11. Education and Leadership

We confess that we have sometimes pursued church growth at the expense of church depth, and divorced evangelism from Christian nurture. We also acknowledge that some of our missions have been too slow to equip and encourage national leaders to assume their rightful responsibilities. Yet we are committed to indigenous principles, and long that every church will have national leaders who manifest a Christian style of leadership in terms not of domination but of service.

We recognize that there is a great need to improve theological education, especially for church leaders. In every nation and culture there should be an effective training program for pastors and laymen in doctrine, discipleship, evangelism, nurture and service. Such training programs should not rely on any stereotyped methodology but should be developed by creative local initiatives according to biblical standards.

12. Spiritual Conflict

We believe that we are engaged in constant spiritual warfare with the principalities and powers of evil, who are seeking to overthrow the church and frustrate its task of world evangelization. We know our need to equip ourselves with God's armor and to fight this battle with the spiritual weapons of truth and prayer. For we detect the activity of our enemy, not only in false ideologies outside the church, but also inside it in false gospels which twist Scripture and put man in the place of God. We need both watchfulness and discernment to safeguard the biblical Gospel.

We acknowledge that we ourselves are not immune to worldliness of thought and action, that is, to a surrender to secularism. For example, although careful studies of church growth, both numerical and spiritual, are right and valuable, we have sometimes neglected them. At other times, desirous to ensure a response to the Gospel, we have compromised our message, manipulated our hearers through pressure techniques, and become unduly preoccupied with statistics or even dishonest in our use of them. All this is worldly. The church must be in the world; the world must not be in the church.

13. Freedom and Persecution

It is the God-appointed duty of every government to secure conditions of peace, justice and liberty in which the church may obey God, serve the Lord Christ, and preach the Gospel without interference. We therefore pray for the leaders of the nations and call upon them to guarantee freedom of thought and conscience, and freedom to practice and propagate religion in accordance with the will of God and as set forth in The Universal Declaration of Human Rights.

We also express our deep concern for all who have been unjustly imprisoned, and especially for our brethren who are suffering for their testimony to the Lord Jesus. We promise to pray and work for their freedom. At the same time we refuse to be intimidated by their fate. God helping us, we too will seek to stand against injustice and to remain faithful to the Gospel, whatever the cost. We do not forget the warnings of Jesus that persecution is inevitable.

14. The Power of the Holy Spirit

We believe in the power of the Holy Spirit. The Father sent his Spirit to bear witness to his Son; without his witness ours is futile. Conviction of sin, faith in Christ, new birth and Christian growth are all his work.

Further, the Holy Spirit is a missionary Spirit; thus evangelism should arise spontaneously from a Spirit-filled church. A church that is not a missionary church is contradicting itself and quenching the Spirit. Worldwide evangelization will become a realistic possibility only when the Spirit renews the church in truth and wisdom, faith, holiness, love and power. We therefore call upon all Christians to pray for such a visitation of the sovereign Spirit of God that all his fruit may appear in all his people and that all his gifts may enrich the body of Christ. Only then will the whole church become a fit instrument in his hands, that the whole earth may hear his voice.

15. The Return of Christ

We believe that Jesus Christ will return personally and visibly, in power and glory, to consummate his salvation and his judgment. This promise of his coming is a further spur to our evangelism, for we remember his words that the Gospel must first be preached to all nations. We believe that the interim period between Christ's ascension and return is to be filled with the mission of the people of God, who have no liberty to stop before the End.

We also remember his warning that false Christs and false prophets will arise as precursors of the final Antichrist. We therefore reject as a proud, self-confident dream the notion that man can ever build a utopia on earth. Our Christian confidence is that God will perfect his kingdom, and we look forward with eager anticipation to that day, and to the new heaven and earth in which righteousness will dwell and God will reign forever.

Meanwhile, we rededicate ourselves to the service of Christ and of men in joyful submission to his authority over the whole of our lives.

Conclusion

Therefore, in the light of this our faith and our resolve, we enter into a solemn covenant with God and with each other, to pray, to plan and to work together for the evangelization of the whole world.

We call upon others to join us. May God help us by his grace and for his glory to be faithful to this our covenant!

Amen, Alleluia!

Appendix B
List, by Region, of the Countries Where the Unreached Peoples Are Located

The following section is designed to help you select a spiritually needy country to be the focus of your evangelistic efforts—whether through prayer, financial support, personal missionary efforts or some combination of the three.

The core of this section is a list, by region, of the 145 countries where the last 5,310 unreached people groups are located. In column two you will find the number of unreached people groups that are predominantly located within the borders of each of these countries. (Source: Frank Kaleb Jansen, General Editor, *A Church for Every People* [Colorado Springs, Colo.: Adopt-A-People Clearinghouse, 1993], with additional information on Turkey and Western Sahara from Terrance J. Riley.)

(*) Indicates the 59 countries from this list that the AD 2000 and Beyond Movement identifies as within the 10/40 window. (Source: Luis Bush, AD 2000.) These are also shown on "The 10/40 Window Countries" map in chapter one.

The third column shows the number of non-Christians projected to be in each of the 145 countries as of mid 1995. This figure is computed using the actual mid-1990 percentage of non-Christians in each country (column four) multiplied by the estimated mid-1995 population for each of those countries. (Source: material collected by Patrick Johnstone, author of *Operation World*, provided in a fax sent to the author, 5/21/93.)

Preceding each regional listing of countries is a map locating the unreached people groups within that region. (Source: Adopt-A-People Clearinghouse; produced by Global Mapping International.) The regions presented first in this listing (for example, Asia, Africa) are generally more afflicted by the "two hungers" than those which follow.

I hope that as you read through this list you are able to appreciate the efforts of the researchers who work so tirelessly to focus the global evangelization campaign. Without their skill and dedication, it would be impossible to provide a list such as this. In fact, this is the first time in history that the unreached peoples could be targeted so precisely.

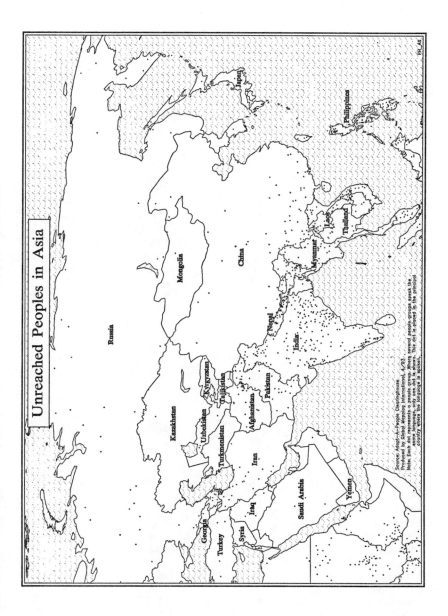

Unreached Peoples in Asia

Sources: Adopt-A-People Clearinghouse.
Produced by Global Mapping International, 4/93.
Note: Each dot represents a people group. Where several people groups speak the same language, only one dot is shown. This dot is placed in the principal country where the language is spoken.

Unreached Peoples in Asia

Country	Number of Unreached People Groups (1993)	Estimated 1995 Non-Christian Population (in millions)	Percent of Non-Christians (1990)
Afghanistan	74	23.10	100.0
Armenia	1	0.71	20.9
Azerbaijian	35	7.40	97.4
*Bahrain	2	0.57	95.0
*Bangladesh	29	131.67	99.6
*Bhutan	14	0.70	99.7
Brunei	3	0.28	94.9
*Cambodia	17	9.16	99.6
*China	104	1140.13	93.9
*Hong Kong	5	5.33	85.9
*India	1,262	910.36	96.1
Indonesia	261	170.95	87.4
*Iran	57	64.24	99.6
*Iraq	18	21.73	97.0
*Israel	7	7.03	97.7
*Japan	2	124.28	98.4
*Jordan	5	3.62	95.3
Kazakhstan	5	15.63	88.8
Korea, North	3	25.35	99.4
*Korea, South	1	29.36	65.4
*Kuwait	7	1.45	97.0
Kyrghyzstan	4	4.35	92.6
*Laos	60	4.53	98.5
*Lebanon	4	2.03	61.6
Malaysia	57	17.80	92.7
Maldives	3	0.20	99.9
Mongolia	13	2.60	99.9
*Myanmar (Burma)	52	43.38	93.7
*Nepal	85	21.37	99.4
*Oman	11	1.67	98.3
*Pakistan	68	139.19	98.3
*Philippines	144	8.04	11.5
*Qatar	4	0.49	97.5
Russia	143	73.04	48.4
*Saudi Arabia	15	16.55	96.8
Singapore	14	2.46	87.7
Sri Lanka	9	16.91	92.4
*Syria	7	13.95	93.6
*Taiwan	11	20.47	95.2
*Tajikistan	6	5.86	97.7
*Thailand	71	59.12	99.2

*Turkey	24	61.08	99.8
*Turkmenistan	15	3.95	96.3
*United Arab Emirates	12	2.02	91.6
Uzbekistan	5	22.98	99.9
*Vietnam	39	67.65	90.2
*Yemen	11	12.4	100.0

Countries in region: 47
Unreached peoples: 2,799
Total non-Christians in the 10/40 countries (*) of this region: 2,956,480,000
Total non-Christians in this region: 3,309,030,000.

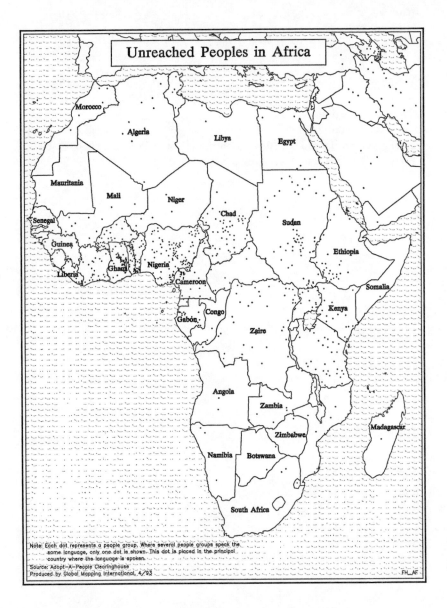

Unreached Peoples in Africa

Note: Each dot represents a people group. Where several people groups speak the same language, only one dot is shown. This dot is placed in the principal country where the language is spoken.

Source: Adopt-A-People Clearinghouse
Produced by Global Mapping International, 4/93

FH_AF

Unreached Peoples in Africa

Country	Number of Unreached People Groups (1993)	Estimated 1995 Non-Christian Population (in millions)	Percent of Non-Christians (1990)
*Algeria	19	29.21	99.7
Angola	7	3.61	31.4
*Benin	23	4.26	76.0
Botswana	3	0.79	52.4
*Burkina Faso	51	9.03	86.8
Burundi	1	1.59	25.3
Cameroon	58	6.94	53.8
Central Africa Rep.	13	1.89	57.3
*Chad	102	5.13	80.2
Comoros Islands	8	0.50	99.4
Congo	8	0.56	24.2
Côte D'Ivoire	40	12.12	79.2
*Djibouti	3	0.49	97.2
*Egypt	11	51.97	85.9
Equatorial Guinea	7	0.11	22.3
Ethiopia	41	25.77	49.0
Gabon	20	0.25	17.8
*Gambia	10	0.97	97.5
Ghana	29	9.75	55.7
*Guinea	19	7.66	98.2
*Guinea Bissau	11	1.03	93.8
Kenya	52	9.36	30.4
Liberia	20	2.25	75.1
*Libya	12	5.28	97.8
Madagascar	5	7.44	52.8
Malawi	8	3.21	32.1
*Mali	26	10.70	98.2
*Mauritania	8	2.29	99.7
Mauritius	5	0.81	67.3
Mayotte	4	0.10	98.0
*Morocco	11	29.04	99.8
Mozambique	17	12.92	72.2
Namibia	6	0.81	37.0
*Niger	26	8.27	99.6
Nigeria	117	59.16	59.1
Reunion	4	0.10	16.5
Rwanda	1	2.06	24.0
Sao Tome & Principe	1	0.01	9.3
*Senegal	21	7.97	94.9
Seychelles	2	0.01	7.6

Sierra Leone	2	4.37	92.9
Somalia	12	8.50	100.0
South Africa	4	10.74	27.4
*Sudan	142	24.91	85.6
Tanzania	48	20.86	63.4
Togo	58	2.84	71.1
*Tunisia	20	8.98	99.8
Uganda	24	6.69	30.4
*Western Sahara	8	0.20	98.6
Zaire	50	3.26	7.7
Zambia	12	4.61	45.2
Zimbabwe	5	5.84	51.2

Countries in region: 52

Unreached peoples: 1,215

Total non-Christians in the 10/40 countries (*) of this region: 207,390,000

Total non-Christians in this region: 416,820,000

(Data for Western Sahara from Barrett and Johnson, *Our Globe and How to Reach It*, p. 127.)

Unreached Peoples in South America

Venezuela
Guyana
Colombia
Ecuador
Peru
Brazil
Bolivia
Paraguay
Uruguay
Argentina
Chile

Source: Adopt-A-People Clearinghouse
Produced by Global Mapping International, 4/93
Note: Each dot represents a people group. Where several people groups speak the
same language, only one dot is shown. This dot is placed in the principal
country where the language is spoken.

FH_SA

Unreached Peoples in South America

Country	Number of Unreached People Groups (1993)	Estimated 1995 Non-Christian Population (in millions)	Percent of Non-Christians (1990)
Argentina	5	3.12	9.1
Bolivia	9	0.97	11.5
Brazil	20	13.70	8.3
Chile	2	1.56	11.0
Colombia	9	1.43	4.1
Ecuador	7	0.92	7.5
Guyana	11	0.41	51.7
Paraguay	19	0.15	3.0
Surinam	3	0.24	60.5
Venezuela	4	2.00	9.0

Countries in region: 10

Unreached peoples: 89

Total non-Christians in this region: 24,500,000

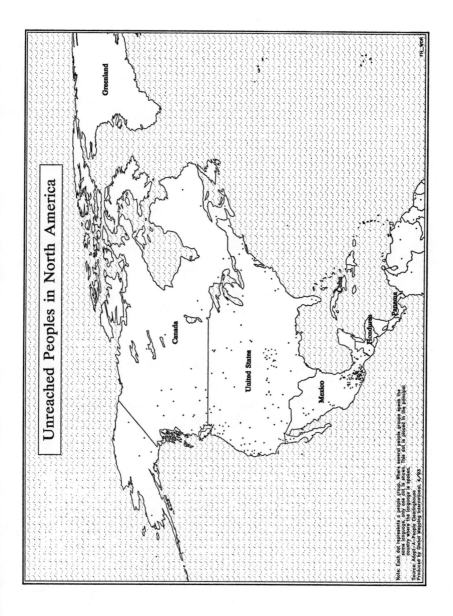

Unreached Peoples in North America

Note: Each dot represents a people group. Where several people groups speak the
same language, one central dot is shown. This dot is placed in the principal
country where the language is spoken.

Source: Adopt-A-People Clearinghouse
Produced by Global Mapping International, 1/93

Unreached Peoples in North America
(including Central America and Caribbean)

Country	Number of Unreached People Groups (1993)	Estimated 1995 Non-Christian Population (in millions)	Percent of Non-Christians (1990)
Belize		0.02	7.9
Canada	57	9.77	35.8
Guatemala	2	1.22	11.5
Mexico	153	11.76	12.0
Panama	1	0.27	10.0
Trinidad & Tobago	1	0.65	43.3
United States	630	71.02	28.5

Countries in region: 7

Unreached peoples: 845

Total non-Christians in this region: 94,710,000

Note: The 630 people groups shown for the United States are primarily composed of the 503 distinct Native American communities in that country, including a large number of native groups in Alaska. The combined population from all of these native groups is less than two million, only about 0.8 percent of the total U.S. population.

Source: John W. Wright, ed., *The Universal Almanac, 1993* (Kansas City: Andrews and McMeel, 1992), pp. 275, 284.

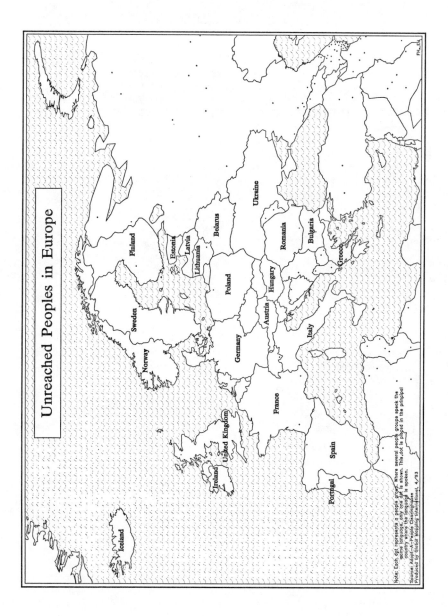

Unreached Peoples in Europe

Iceland
Norway
Sweden
Finland
Estonia
Latvia
Lithuania
Ireland
United Kingdom
Germany
Poland
Belarus
Ukraine
France
Austria
Hungary
Romania
Bulgaria
Italy
Greece
Spain
Portugal

Note: Each dot represents a people group. Where several people groups speak the
same language, only one dot is shown. This dot is placed in the principal
country where the language is spoken.
Source: Adopt-A-People Clearinghouse
Produced by Global Mapping International, 4/93

Unreached Peoples in Europe

Country	Number of Unreached People Groups (1993)	Estimated 1995 Non-Christian Population (in millions)	Percent of Non-Christians (1990)
Albania	4	3.0	85.8
Austria	2	0.73	9.7
Belgium	3	1.05	10.5
Bulgaria	11	2.79	31.0
Finland	5	0.54	10.8
France	18	16.63	28.9
Germany	4	21.04	26.3
*Greece	2	0.38	3.8
Ireland	1	0.39	10.1
Italy	5	11.29	19.6
Moldova	4	1.66	36.9
Netherlands	13	5.49	35.9
Poland	1	0.83	2.1
*Portugal	1	0.89	8.6
Romania	2	3.57	15.0
Spain	2	4.93	12.3
Sweden	2	3.39	40.8
Switzerland	2	0.59	9.0
United Kingdom	12	19.2	33.5
Yugoslavia	8	2.68	26.0

Countries in region: 20

Unreached peoples: 102

Total non-Christians in the 10/40 countries (*) of this region: 1,270,000

Total non-Christians in this region: 101,070,000

Unreached Peoples in Australia and Oceania

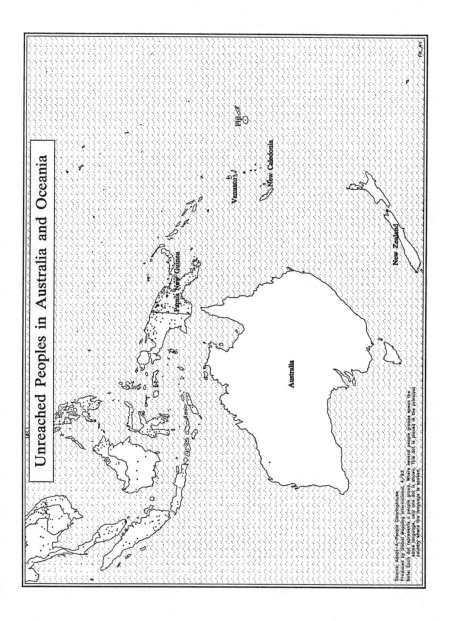

Papua New Guinea

Vanuatu

New Caledonia

Fiji

Australia

New Zealand

Source: Adopt-A-People Clearinghouse.
Produced by Global Mapping International, 4/93
Note: Each dot represents a people group. Where several people groups speak the
same language, only one dot is shown. The dot is placed in the principal
country where the language is spoken.

Unreached Peoples in Australia and Oceania

Country	Number of Unreached People Groups (1993)	Estimated 1995 Non-Christian Population (in millions)	Percent of Non-Christians (1990)
Australia	5	6.85	38.70
Cook Islands	1	0.00	10.00
Fiji	2	0.38	46.90
French Polynesia	5	0.03	15.60
Micronesia	3	0.02	19.00
New Caledonia	7	0.04	21.00
Papua New Guinea	228	0.85	18.40
Vanuatu	8	0.05	25.80
Wallis and Fortuna	1	0.00	0.90

Countries in region: 9
Unreached peoples: 260
Total non-Christians in this region: 8,220,000

Appendix C
A Call to Action: An Appeal to Disciples Everywhere

The following was adopted at the second Adopt-A-People Consultation in April 1993. It is included here to demonstrate the synergistic power of the church universal as it works cooperatively to obey the Great Commission.

Introduction
We, the 230 participants at the Second Adopt-A-People Consultation, meeting in Colorado Springs, USA, April 25-27, 1993, make the following appeal to *fellow disciples everywhere*. We come from more than 107 churches, denominations, mission agencies and other Christian organizations, and included some participants from other countries. We met to consider the goal of a church for every people by the year 2000. God strongly impressed upon us the need for *prayer mobilization* and *unity* along the pathway to that goal.

The appeal has two sections: *shared convictions* and *ongoing recommendations*. With God's help we believe that a church for every people by the year 2000 is an attainable goal. We do not believe that the date of this goal is necessarily the precise time of the return of Christ nor do we predict certain success by that date but we are convinced that it is a goal that still can be accomplished by the enabling grace of God.

Our Shared Convictions
1. We recognize the reaching of unreached peoples is primarily and ultimately a spiritual battle in which God's grace and power are indispensable.

2. We affirm the goal of a church for every people is essential in making the Gospel accessible to every person by the year 2000.

3. We rejoice in reports of God's sovereignty expressed through peoples reached for Christ. They strengthen our faith, increase our hope and galvanize our commitment to a church for every people.

4. We recognize that we have not done all that we could in making Christ

known to the unreached peoples. For this we repent.

5. We celebrate our love for Christ by commitment to Him and to His Great Commission, a bond which draws us together to find ways to accelerate the establishment of spiritually vital churches among every people.

6. As we approach the year 2000 we recognize that God has placed Christians in a time of unprecedented opportunity created by the opening of restricted access countries, dedicated prayer networks, and the availability and widespread distribution of the Word of God and other gospel resources.

7. We celebrate the growth, vitality and missionary endeavors of the Two-thirds World Church. We recognize their crucial role as full partners in the attainment of the goal.

8. We recognize that research information is essential for concerted prayer and to design appropriate strategies to establish Christ's church among every people.

9. We believe that a focused attention on unreached peoples requires churches, denominations and missionary agencies to set new priorities in the use of finances, deployment of personnel and strategic focus of energies.

10. We rejoice in the strategic opportunities that all believers now have to champion the cause of the unreached peoples.

11. We realize that our common love for the Lord Jesus Christ and trust in His finished work on Calvary, combined with our desire to work together toward our AD 2000 goal, are stronger than the differences that tend to divide us.

12. We praise God for the growing prayer movement for unreached peoples.

13. We rejoice in the imminent availability of the Registry of Peoples and Languages (ROPAL) information to researchers as a tool in the development of unreached people strategies.

14. We rejoice in the formation of the Peoples Information Network (PIN) and encourage mission agencies to participate in the network.

15. We affirm the diligent, persevering initiatives taken by the Adopt-A-People Clearing House and express our gratitude to them for calling this consultation.

16. We rejoice that the Unreached and Adoptable Peoples listing has been issued as a working document and encourage individuals and agencies everywhere to continue efforts to update and improve it.

17. We rejoice in the cooperation and unity that is evident in our midst and the firm conviction that the task can be done by working together in reliance upon the grace and power of God.

18. We hold that each participant in this conference is a voice for the

voiceless peoples and their representative to seek to focus energy, budget and personnel for these unreached peoples.

Recommendations for Practical Steps to Accomplish the Goal

1. Encourage the mobilization of Christians in all countries, regions and continents of the world to take up the challenge of reaching the unreached peoples of our world.

2. Seek increased participation of our churches and agencies in prayer mobilization focused on the unreached peoples of the world, noting two special prayer events: Praying Through the 10/40 Window in October 1993 and the Day to Change the World on June 25, 1994.

3. Encourage mission agencies from the developed world to seek partnership with similar agencies from the Two-thirds world in planning new strategies towards reaching the unreached peoples of the world by the year 2000.

4. Encourage every mission agency and church group to continue research and input to the Peoples Information Network (PIN) about the stage of "reachedness" of peoples within their ministry areas.

5. Encourage deployment of an increasing percentage of our resources for work among unreached peoples.

6. Commit ourselves to cooperate with the Adopt-A-People Clearing House in the production of profiles for the intercessory prayer movement.

7. Increase support to make research functions operational in each country that will provide current, accurate information on the status of reaching a people.

8. Encourage mission agencies and churches to make the most effective use of local and global resources to accomplish the goal.

9. Encourage the development of catalization resources to mobilize local churches to adopt unreached peoples.

10. Encourage local churches to take steps in relation to their commitment to world evangelization such as, (1) *recognize* the high priority of the unreached people groups, (2) *establish* a budgetary process whereby they can contribute to this kind of outreach, (3) *encourage* weekly or monthly fellowship for those who wish to pray and work toward this goal, (4) *accept* the challenge of the local congregation adopting an unreached people group by working through a specific denominational or interdenominational mission agency, and (5) *seek* to pass on the passion for the unreached people to three or more other congregations.

11. Within a year plan to hold a small working consultation to address remaining issues and strengthen implementation strategies.

Notes

Introduction

[1] Fax from David B. Barrett, June 7, 1993.

[2] See details in chapter two.

[3] Luis Bush, *Getting to the Core of the Core: The 10/40 Window* (San Jose, Calif.: Partners International, 1990).

[4] Scripture quotations in this book are taken from the New International Version. Scriptural references will always be provided within the text, so that readers can readily make comparisons with the version of their choice.

[5] David B. Barrett and Todd M. Johnson, *Our Globe and How to Reach It: Seeing the World Evangelized by AD 2000 and Beyond* (Birmingham, Ala.: New Hope, 1990), p. 27.

[6] Readers familiar with the diplomatic world will recognize the term "special envoy" as coming from that arena. It seems to me that some of the skills of expert diplomats will be required by God's Special Envoys.

Chapter 1

[1] David B. Barrett, *World Christian Encyclopedia: A Comparative Study of Churches and Religions in the Modern World, AD 1900—2000* (Nairobi: Oxford University Press, 1982), p. 3.

[2] Ibid., p. 826.

[3] David Barrett and Todd Johnson, in a helpful typology, conceptualize all of the world's countries as broken into three groups. The "A," *Unevangelized* world is composed of the 30 countries that are 50 percent or less evangelized. The "B," *Evangelized, non-Christian* world is composed of the 76 countries that are more than 50 percent evangelized but less than 60 percent professing Christian. The "C," *Christian* world is composed of the 145 countries that are at least 60 percent Christian and 95 percent or more evangelized. (Barrett and Johnson, *Our Globe and How to Reach It: Seeing the World Evangelized by AD 2000 and Beyond* [Birmingham, Ala.: New Hope, 1990], pp. 26, 126.)

[4] Frank Kaleb Jansen, ed., *A Church for Every People: The List of Unreached and*

Adoptable Peoples (Colorado Springs, Colo.: Adopt-A-People Clearinghouse, 1993).

[5]John A. Holzmann, "1.3 Billion 'UNEVANGELIZED' or 2.4 Billion 'UN-REACHED,'" *Mission Frontiers*, August-September 1985, p. 21.

[6]Chapter six will discuss ways of measuring the restrictiveness of various countries, plus techniques Special Envoys can use to maximize their effectiveness under differing kinds of opportunities and restrictions.

[7]Jansen, ed., *A Church for Every People.*

[8]The total non-Christian population of the world in 1995 is estimated at four billion. This estimate is based on the latest possible data included in an advance copy of Patrick Johnstone's *Operation World*, received May 21, 1993. I take his 1990 estimate of the percentage of non-Christians in the world (69.9 percent) and multiply this by his estimate of the 1995 total world population, 5,757,300,000. Result: 4,024,352,700 non-Christians in 1995.

[9]AD 2000 and Beyond Movement, Assessment Task Force, definition updated March 14, 1993.

[10]Luis Bush, *Getting to the Core of the Core: The 10/40 Window* (San Jose, Calif.: Partners International, 1990).

[11]The list of least-developed countries is assembled by the United Nations and is based on their gross domestic product (GDP). Quoted in Frank Kaleb Jansen, "Least Developed Countries," in Frank Kaleb Jansen, ed., *Target Earth: The Necessity of Diversity in a Holistic Perspective on World Mission* (Kailua-Kona, Hawaii: University of the Nations, 1989), pp. 80-81.

[12]Ralph Winter, "Editorial," *Mission Frontiers*, April-May 1991, pp. 2, 4.

[13]For the latest report on restricted countries, contact Issachar (Frontier Missions Strategies), P.O. Box 6788, Lynnwood, WA 98036, and ask for their latest *Restricted World Ministry Handbook.*

[14]Barrett and Johnson, *Our Globe and How to Reach It*, p. 27.

[15]Thanks to David Barrett for the suggestion that I expand on this point. Telephone conversation, June 10, 1993.

[16]Barrett and Johnson, *Our Globe and How to Reach It*, pp. 27, 29, 30, 32.

Chapter 2

[1]David B. Barrett and Todd M. Johnson, *Our Globe and How to Reach It: Seeing the World Evangelized by AD 2000 and Beyond* (Birmingham, Ala: New Hope, 1990), p. vi.

[2]Berry Fiess, "Jesus Film Project" update, received by fax, March 5, 1993.

[3]Barrett and Johnson, *Our Globe and How to Reach It*, p. 27.

[4]David Barrett, personal communication with the author, March 16, 1993.

[5]Barrett and Johnson, *Our Globe and How to Reach It*, p. 27.

[6]J. Christy Wilson Jr., quoted in Sharon E. Mumper, "New Strategies to Evangelize Muslims Gain Effectiveness," *Christianity Today*, May 17, 1985, p. 17.

[7]Ralph Winter, telephone conversation, July 11, 1993.

[8]David B. Barrett, "Annual Statistical Table on Global Mission: 1993," *International Bulletin of Missionary Research,* January 1993, p. 23.

Chapter 3

[1]In mid 1993 there were actually some 616 million Great Commission, Bible-believing Christians in the world. This computes to 1,026 evangelical Christians for every Special Envoy. (David B. Barrett and Todd M. Johnson, *International Bulletin of Missionary Research,* January 1993, p. 2.)

[2]David B. Barrett and Todd M. Johnson, *Our Globe and How to Reach It: Seeing the World Evangelized by AD 2000 and Beyond* (Birmingham, Ala: New Hope, 1990), p. 27.

[3]Ibid.

Chapter 4

[1]For students interested in such areas as history, political science, anthropology, sociology, botany and a variety of other fields, the opportunity to study in an unreached people group might produce a wealth of rare knowledge and even valuable expertise.

[2]The 1990 Desert Storm Campaign in Saudi Arabia placed thousands of Western Christians in positions where they could build connections to unreached peoples. Likewise military/humanitarian campaigns in other restricted-access countries (such as Somalia in 1992) have produced similar ties. What is required, therefore, is for these short-term visitors to convert to longer-term resident status. In this effort, they may be able to employ some of the peaceful skills that had originally attracted the host country to them.

[3]To further explore the impacts of syncretism and relativism, see the articles by Peter Beyerhaus and Donald McGavran on these subjects in Tetsunao Yamamori and Charles R. Taber, eds., *Christopaganism or Indigenous Christianity?* (South Pasadena, Calif.: William Carey Library, 1975).

[4]Unanimously voted by the United Nations, 1948 (the USSR and Saudi Arabia abstaining).

[5]Sam Wilson and Gordon Aeschliman, "The Hidden Half," quoted in *Mission Frontiers,* August-September, 1985, p. 17.

[6]Gordon Aeschliman, "Anyone Love a Russian?" *World Christian,* January-February, 1985, p. 6.

[7]Ray A. Giles, "To Fulfill the Task," in Doug Priest Jr., ed., *Unto the Uttermost* (Pasadena: William Carey Library, 1984), p. 303.

[8]"Summary of Report #1" taken from the Hamilton Tentmaker Survey published by TMQ Research (Don Hamilton, director).

Chapter 5

[1]For a helpful article on this technique see Hal Guffey's "Reach the World Without Leaving Campus—Share the 'Good News' With Internationals" in *The Great Commission Handbook 1984* (Evanston, Ill.: Sherman Marketing, Center for

Information on Christian Students' Opportunities, 1984), pp. 45-50.

Chapter 6
[1]Through the efforts of Frank Kaleb Jansen, Luis Bush, Ron Rowland, Clark Scanlon, Terrance J. Riley and many others. For some of these other names, see Frank Kaleb Jansen, ed., *A Church for Every People: The List of Unreached and Adoptable Peoples* (Colorado Springs, Colo.: Adopt-A-People Clearinghouse, 1993).

[2]See David B. Barrett and J. W. Reapsome, *Seven Hundred Plans to Evangelize the World: The Rise of a Global Evangelization Movement* (Birmingham, Ala.: New Hope, 1988).

[3]This ratio is based on dividing the estimated number of physically hungry non-Christians in the last unreached people groups by the hoped-for size of the Special Envoys force. Specific ratios will vary, of course, depending on how many Envoys are sent to a given group. In any case, however, the challenge will be enormous, with odds reminiscent of the biblical encounters.

[4]Donald McGavran, *The Bridges of God* (New York: Friendship Press, 1955), p. 1.

[5]Personal conversation with the author, June 11, 1993.

[6]McGavran, *Bridges*.

[7]Carl Lawrence, *The Church in China* (Minneapolis: Bethany House, 1985), pp. 23-161.

[8]Peter McPherson, United States Agency for International Development. Note: The 1985 World Population Data Sheet indicates a lower estimate (79.3 percent) for the portion of the world's people living in less-developed countries in the year 2000; but whether the 90 percent or 79.3 percent estimate turns out to be most accurate, the statement made in the text will still be correct.

[9]C. Peter Wagner, "Three Growth Principles for a Soul-winning Church," in Elmer L. Towns, John N. Vaughan and David J. Seifert, eds., *The Complete Book of Church Growth* (Wheaton, Ill.: Tyndale House, 1981), pp. 279-83.

[10]Ibid., p. 280.

[11]Ibid., p. 281.

[12]Ibid., p. 282.

[13]David B. Barrett and Todd M. Johnson, *Our Globe and How to Reach It: Seeing the World Evangelized by AD 2000 and Beyond* (Birmingham, Ala.: New Hope, 1990), p. 27.

[14]Jelet Fryman, "From the Uttermost Parts," *World Christian*, March-April 1985, p. 28.

[15]C. Peter Wagner, *The Crest of the Wave* (Ventura, Calif.: Regal, 1983), pp. 279-83.

[16]Larry D. Pate, *From Every People: A Handbook of Two-Thirds World Missions with Directory/Histories/Analysis* (Monrovia, Calif.: MARC, 1989), p. 52.

[17]Roland Allen, *The Spontaneous Expansion of the Church* (Grand Rapids, Mich.:

Eerdmans, 1962), p. 143.

[18]Joseph C. Aldrich, *Life-Style Evangelism* (Portland, Ore.: Multnomah Press, 1981), p. 75.

[19]*Gyo'yeuk Back'suh* (South Korea: Gyo'yeuk Yongu'so, 1989); Pure Gospel Education Book, published by the Pure Gospel Education Institute.

[20]Howard Brant, "Community Development Among Muslims," a paper presented at the Symbiotic Ministries Symposium, Biola University, March 6-7, 1985.

[21]Paul J. L. Bergsma, "Holistic Urban Ministry in Tegucigalpa, Honduras," *Urban Mission,* January 1984, pp. 40-42.

[22]Brother Andrew, *The Ethics of Smuggling* (Wheaton, Ill.: Tyndale House, 1974).

Chapter 7

[1]Art Beals with Larry Libby, *Beyond Hunger: A Biblical Mandate for Social Responsibility* (Portland, Ore.: Multnomah Press, 1985), p. 189.

[2]Excerpts in this section are from John Huffaker, "Symbiosis: A Muslim Case-study," a paper submitted for the Symbiotic Ministries Symposium, Biola University, March 6, 1985.

[3]Such delayed fruits are the natural result of the preparatory evangelism Special Envoys will need to practice in many of the unreached people groups.

[4]Ted W. Engstrom, in a letter quoted in *Christianity Today,* October 18, 1985, p. 7.

[5]Beals, *Beyond Hunger,* p. 15.

[6]*Global 2000* is by the President's Commission on the Year 2000.

[7]For more statistics about global hunger, request a free copy of *The Hunger Primer,* published by Food for the Hungry, P.O. Box E, Scottsdale, Arizona 85252.

[8]Tom Sine, "Development: Its Secular Past and Its Uncertain Future," in *The Church in Response to Human Need,* ed. Tom Sine (Monrovia, Calif.: MARC, 1983), p. 13.

[9]From an interview with the Reverend George Bajenski, November 22, 1985.

[10]Arthur Simon, interviewed by Barbara R. Thompson in *Christianity Today,* September 6, 1985.

[11]Jerry Bedsole, Southern Baptist missionary veterinarian to Ethiopia, quoted in *Baptist Beacon,* September 5, 1985, p. 5.

[12]James B. Wyngaarden, M.D., and Lloyd H. Smith Jr., M.D., eds., *Textbook of Medicine* (Philadelphia: W. B. Saunders, 1982), 2:1363-67; and Joan Graf, "Death by Fasting," *Science 81,* November 1981, p. 18.

[13]Brother Andrew, John and Elizabeth Sherrill, *God's Smuggler* (Carmel, N.Y.: Guideposts, 1967).

[14]Cliff Westergren, "Priests On the Street Corners of the World," a paper presented at the Symbiotic Ministries Symposium, Biola University, March 6-7, 1985.

[15]Miriam Adeney, *God's Foreign Policy* (Grand Rapids, Mich.: Eerdmans, 1984), pp. 25-26.
[16]Ibid., pp. 23-24.
[17]Beals, *Beyond Hunger*, p. 75.
[18]Ibid.
[19]David B. Barrett and Todd M. Johnson, *Our Globe and How to Reach It: Seeing the World Evangelized by AD 2000 and Beyond* (Birmingham, Ala.: New Hope, 1990), p. 28.

Chapter 8

[1]Howard Brant, "Integrating Development with Church Planting," a paper submitted for the Symbiotic Ministries Symposium at Biola University, March 6-7, 1985.
[2]For various approaches to development, see David C. Korten, *Getting to the 21st Century: Voluntary Action and the Global Agenda* (West Hartford, Conn.: Kumarian Press, 1990).
[3]Donald McGavran, *Eye of the Storm: The Great Debate in Mission* (Waco, Tex.: Word, 1972).
[4]These obviously are abbreviated definitions of two very important concepts. For the full definitions see my article, "Toward the Symbiotic Ministry: God's Mandate for the Church Today," in *Missiology, An International Review* 5, no. 3 (1977).
[5]J. Linsley Gressit, "Symbiosis Runs Wild on the Backs of High-Living Weevils," *Smithsonian* 7, no. 11, (1977), pp. 136-38.
[6]Ibid., p. 136.
[7]Letter to the author from Jerry Ballard, executive director, World Relief, 1985.

Chapter 9

[1]*Webster's Ninth New Collegiate Dictionary* (Springfield, Mass.: Merriam-Webster, 1989).
[2]For example, Stephen R. Covey, *Principle Centered Leadership* (New York: Summit, 1990); Harper W. Boyd Jr. and Orville C. Walker Jr., *Marketing Management: A Strategic Approach* (Homewood, Ill.: Irwin, 1990).
[3]For a more detailed exploration of "Paul's strategy," see Roland Allen, *Missionary Methods: St. Paul's or Ours?* (Grand Rapids, Mich.: Eerdmans, 1962).
[4]Craig Michalski, "Coming of Age: Tentmaking Is Not Just for Apostles Anymore," *World Christian*, May-June 1985, p. 36.

Chapter 10

[1]Jane Allyn Piliavin and Peter L. Callero, *Giving Blood: The Development of an Altruistic Personality* (Baltimore, Md.: Johns Hopkins University Press, 1991).
[2]Ibid.
[3]Source of the half a million figure, Gordon Loux, International Students,

Inc., Colorado Springs, Colo., in fax received March 11, 1993. Source of the 34,000 figure: The Institute of International Education and *U.S. News and World Report*, quoted by Hal Guffey in "Reach the World Without Leaving Campus—Share the 'Good News' with Internationals," in *The Great Commission Handbook 1984* (Evanston, Ill.: Sherman Marketing, Center for Information on Christian Students' Opportunities, 1984), p. 45.

[4]For more information on this subject see Tetsunao Yamamori, "Reaching Ethnic America," *Church Growth: America,* November-December 1978, pp. 4-6, 14-15.

Chapter 11

[1]This figure is based on the latest possible data included in an advance copy of Patrick Johnstone's *Operation World.* See footnote 18 in chapter one.

[2]The 80 percent estimate for the world's non-Christians living in the 10/40 window again draws on Patrick Johnstone's data. Here, however, I added all the Christians he estimates to be in the AD 2000 and Beyond Movement's list of 10/40 window countries. The "nearly 80 percent" figure is this total divided by the estimated number of non-Christians expected to be in the world in 1995.

Bibliography

Among the books that God's Special Envoys may find especially valuable are these:

Miriam Adeney's *God's Foreign Policy* (Grand Rapids, Mich.: Eerdmans, 1984) is an excellent introduction to the complexities of trying to do good in foreign cultures. Although I would not agree with all of Adeney's evaluations of specific development techniques, I believe her book will give the prospective Envoy valuable insights and an appreciation of the necessity of approaching each culture on its own terms.

Roland Allen's *The Spontaneous Expansion of the Church* (Grand Rapids, Mich.: Eerdmans, 1962) is a mature work by a very insightful missiologist. First published in 1932, it has withstood the test of time. Although some of Allen's language may seem a little dated, he has brilliant insights into the techniques that make spontaneous expansion work.

God's Smuggler by Brother Andrew and John and Elizabeth Sherrill (Carmel, N.Y.: Guideposts Associates, 1967) is a classic, and deservedly so. As a book about the adventure of missions and the joy of giving one's full trust to the Lord, this volume is hard to beat.

Beyond Hunger by Art Beals with Larry Libby (Portland, Ore.: Multnomah Press, 1985) provides a host of valuable examples of the symbiotic ministry in action. This is good reading for those who are contemplating work with symbiotic ministries—focusing on both physical and spiritual need.

Carl Lawrence's *The Church in China* (Minneapolis: Bethany House, 1985) is full of inspiring stories that demonstrate the true dynamism and miraculous nature of Christ's church in a highly repressive land.

Norman Rohrer's *This Poor Man Cried* (Wheaton, Ill.: Tyndale House, 1985) is a true story of a pioneer in the Christian relief and development field, Dr. Larry Ward. It will inspire you, and also help your understanding of the enormity of some of the problems God's Special Envoys will face.

Today's Tentmakers by J. Christy Wilson Jr. (Seattle: Overseas Counseling Service, 1979) provides an alternative model for worldwide witness. Just as the apostle Paul financed his own ministry by tentmaking, today's tentmakers can make an invaluable contribution to world evangelization, being free to reach restricted-access countries, and easing financial burdens upon the church.

There are also a number of other works consulted in preparation of this book that Special Envoys might find especially valuable in their preparations to enter the mission field. These include the following.

Books

Aldrich, Joseph C. *Life-Style Evangelism*. Portland, Ore.: Multnomah Press, 1981.

Andrew, Brother. *The Ethics of Smuggling*. Wheaton, Ill.: Tyndale House, 1974.

Barrett, David B., ed. *World Christian Encyclopedia: A Comparative Study of Churches and Religions in the Modern World, AD 1900—2000*. Nairobi: Oxford University Press, 1982.

Barrett, David B., and Todd M. Johnson. *Our Globe and How to Reach It: Seeing the World Evangelized by AD 2000 and Beyond* ("A Manual for the Decade of Evangelization, 1990—2000"). Birmingham, Ala.: New Hope, 1990.

Barrett, David B., and J. W. Reapsome. *Seven Hundred Plans to Evangelize the World: The Rise of a Global Evangelization Movement*. Birmingham, Ala.: New Hope, 1988.

Bush, Luis, ed. *AD 2000 and Beyond Handbook: A Church for Every People and the Gospel for Every Person by AD 2000*. AD 2000 and Beyond Movement, 1992.

Conn, Harvie M., ed. *Reaching the Unreached: The Old-New Challenge*. Phillipsburg, N.J.: Presbyterian and Reformed, 1984.

Dayton, Edward R., and Samuel Wilson, eds. *The Refugees Among Us: Unreached Peoples '83*. Monrovia, Calif.: MARC, 1983.

Ending Hunger: An Idea Whose Time Has Come. New York: Praeger, 1985.

Jansen, Frank Kaleb, ed. *A Church for Every People: The List of Unreached and Adoptable Peoples*. Colorado Springs, Colo.: Adopt-A-People Clearinghouse, 1993. Copublished with the AD 2000 and Beyond Movement, MARC (Mission Advance Research and Communication Center), Southern Baptist Convention—Foreign Mission Board, SIL (Summer Institute of Linguistics) and U.S. Center for World Mission.

Jansen, Frank Kaleb, ed. *Target Earth: The Necessity of Diversity in a Holistic Perspective on World Mission*. Kailua-Kona, Hawaii: University of the Nations and Pasadena, Calif.: Global Mapping International, 1989.

Millham, Doug. *Lake Wales Consultation Manual*. Monrovia, Calif.: MARC, 1986.

Otis, George Jr. *The Last of the Giants: Lifting the Veil on Islam and the End Times*. Tarrytown, N.Y.: Chosen Books, 1991.

Priest, Doug Jr., ed. *Unto the Uttermost*. Pasadena: William Carey Library, 1984.

Restricted World Ministry Handbook: A Special Report on the Nations of the Restricted-Access World. Lynwood, Wash.: Issachar Frontier Missions Strategies, 1989.

Samovar, Larry A., and Richard E. Porter. *Intercultural Communication: A Reader*. Belmont, Calif.: Wadsworth, 1976.

Stott, John. *Lausanne Occasional Papers, Number 3*. Minneapolis: World Wide Publications, 1975.

Towns, Elmer, John N. Vaughn and David J. Seifert. *The Complete Book of Church Growth*. Wheaton, Ill.: Tyndale House, 1981.

Ward, Larry. *And There Will Be Famines.* Ventura, Calif.: Gospel Light, 1983.

Wilson, J. Christy. *Introducing Islam.* New York: Friendship Press, n.d.

Winter, Ralph D., and Steven C. Hawthorne, eds. *Perspectives on the World Christian Movement: A Reader.* Revised edition. Pasadena, Calif.: William Carey Library, 1992.

Yamamori, Tetsunao. *Church Growth in Japan.* South Pasadena, Calif.: William Carey Library, 1974.

Yamamori, Tetsunao, and E. LeRoy Lawson. *Church Growth: Everybody's Business.* Cincinnati: Standard Publishing, 1975.

Yamamori, Tetsunao, and E. LeRoy Lawson. *Introducing Church Growth.* Cincinnati: Standard Publishing, 1975.

Yamamori, Tetsunao, and Charles R. Taber, eds. *Christopaganism or Indigenous Christianity?* South Pasadena, Calif.: William Carey Library, 1975.

Periodicals

Barrett, David B., and Todd M. Johnson, eds. *AD 2000 Global Monitor.* ("A monthly trends newsletter measuring progress in world evangelization into the 21st century.")

The Great Commission Handbook 1984. Evanston, Ill.: Sherman Marketing Services, 1984.

International and Intercultural Communication Annual. Vol. 5 (1979). Falls Church, Va.: Speech Communication Association.

Leadership. Spring 1984.

Mission Frontiers.

Stewardship Journal. ("A Christian review about obedient use of resources.") Vol. 2, nos. 3 & 4 (Fall/Summer 1992).

Symbiosis. October 1985.

Urban Mission. Vol. 1, no. 3 (1984).

World Christian. January-December 1985.

Articles and Brochures

Brant, Howard. "Integrating Development with Church Planting."

Bush, Luis. Getting to the Core of the Core: The 10/40 Window. San Jose, Calif.: Partners International, 1990.

Otis, George Jr., and the Sentinal Group Staff. "The Holy Spirit Around the World." Charisma and Christian Life 18, no. 6 (1993): 19-74.

Westergren, Cliff. "Priests on the Street Corners of the World."

Yamamori, Tetsunao. "Toward the Symbiotic Ministry: God's Mandate for the Church Today." *Missiology, An International Review* 5, no. 3 (1977).

_____. "Factors in Church Growth in the U.S."

Another publication that would be helpful for God's Special Envoys is the "Christian Life and Witness Course"—a helpful first step for those who have never witnessed before. Available from Billy Graham Evangelistic Association, P.O. Box 779, Minneapolis, MN 55440.

About the Author

Tetsunao Yamamori is president of Food for the Hungry International (FHI), a Christian relief and development organization currently providing physical and spiritual assistance to a million people in more than twenty countries. Founded in 1971, FHI is headquartered in Geneva, Switzerland. It has support offices in six countries (Canada, Japan, Korea, Norway, the United Kingdom and the United States) and works in synergistic partnership with more than 300,000 prayer warriors, thousands of churches and with dozens of government and private agencies.

Dr. Yamamori was born in Nagoya, Japan, where he received his early education. After moving to the United States he obtained a B.D. from Texas Christian University and a Ph.D. (in sociology of religion) from Duke University.

Before joining Food for the Hungry in 1981, Dr. Yamamori taught in colleges and universities for eighteen years. During this time he served as professor and director of Intercultural Studies at Biola University, as vice president of the Institute for American Church Growth, and as dean of Northwest Christian College.

Dr. Yamamori has written several books, numerous articles, and at least a dozen book chapters in the fields of missiology, sociology and international development. He currently serves as an adjunct professor of sociology at Arizona State University.

A personal survivor of near starvation as a child in Japan during World War II, Dr. Yamamori is tireless in helping those who suffer from physical and spiritual hunger. He visits many of the world's neediest regions each year.

Also by Tetsunao Yamamori:

Christopaganism or Indigenous Christianity? (edited with Charles R. Taber, William Carey Library)

Church Growth: Everybody's Business (with LeRoy Lawson, Standard Publishing)

Church Growth in Japan (William Carey Library)

Exploring Religious Meaning (with others; Prentice Hall/Simon and Schuster)

God's New Envoys (Multnomah Press)

Growing Our Future: Food Security and the Environment (edited with Katie Smith, Kumarian Press)

Introducing Church Growth (with LeRoy Lawson, Standard Publishing)